MY FATHER'S HOUSE

MY FATHER'S HOUSE

Yigal Allon

Translated from the Hebrew by
Reuven Ben-Yosef

Illustrated by Shirley Hirsch

W · W · NORTON & COMPANY · INC ·
New York

FIRST EDITION

Library of Congress Cataloging in Publication Data

Allon, Yigal, 1918–
My father's house.

Translation of Bet avi.
1. Allon, Yigal, 1918– 2. Paikovits family.
I. Title.
DS126.6.A49A3213 956.94'05'0924 [B] 75-43945
ISBN 0-393-07498-6

Published simultaneously in Canada
by George J. McLeod Limited, Toronto

PRINTED IN THE UNITED STATES OF AMERICA
1 2 3 4 5 6 7 8 9 0

For my children,
Yiftach and Goni

By Way of Introduction

I WANTED very much to describe Israel as it appeared in the latter part of the nineteenth century, when my parents' parents, together with the other pioneers of their generation, began rebuilding and resettling the neglected, underpopulated country. However, the only way I could do this was by hearsay or by researching the writings and descriptions of those heroic days. Although I surely could have kept to a truthful and objective view, I thought it might be better to single out a description of the country as composed by an eyewitness who had traveled in Israel, observed it and put his findings into words. I found no more impressive, authentic description than that of Mark Twain, who visited the Holy Land in 1867 and recorded his impressions in *The Innocents Abroad:*

> At noon we took a swim in the Sea of Galilee . . . a lake six miles wide and neutral in color; with steep green banks, unrelieved by shrubbery . . . its prominent feature, one tree. No ingenuity could make such a picture beautiful. . . .
>
> Magdala is not a beautiful place. It is thoroughly Syrian, and that is to say that it is thoroughly ugly, and cramped, squalid, uncomfortable, and filthy. . . . The streets of Magdala

are anywhere from three to six feet wide, and reeking with uncleanliness. The houses are from five to seven feet high, and all built upon one arbitrary plan—the ungraceful form of a drygoods box. The sides are daubed with a smooth white plaster, and tastefully frescoed aloft and alow with disks of camel-dung placed there to dry. This gives the edifice the romantic appearance of having been riddled with cannon-balls, and imparts to it a very warlike aspect. . . .

As we rode into Magdala * not a soul was visible. But the ring of the horses' hoofs roused the stupid population, and they all came trooping out—old men and old women, boys and girls, the blind, the crazy, and the crippled, all in ragged, soiled, and scanty raiment, and all abject beggars by nature, instinct, and education. How the vermin-tortured vagabonds did swarm! How they showed their scars and sores, and piteously pointed to their maimed and crooked limbs, and begged with their pleading eyes for charity! We had invoked a spirit we could not lay. They hung to the horses' tails, clung to their manes and the stirrups, closed in on every side in scorn of dangerous hoofs—and out of their infidel throats, with one accord, burst an agonizing and most infernal chorus: "Howajji, bucksheesh! howajji, bucksheesh! howajji, bucksheesh! bucksheesh! bucksheesh!" I never was in a storm like that before. . . .

We reached Tabor safely, and considerably in advance of that old iron-clad swindle of a guard. We never saw a human being on the whole

* A town on the shore of the Sea of Galilee.

route, much less lawless hordes of Bedouins. Tabor stands solitary and alone, a giant sentinel above the Plain of Esdraelon. It rises some fourteen hundred feet above the surrounding level, a green, wooded cone, symmetrical and full of grace—a prominent landmark, and one that is exceedingly pleasant to eyes surfeited with the repulsive monotony of desert Syria. . . .

Arriving at the furthest verge of the Plain, we rode a little way up a hill and found ourselves at Endor, famous for its witch. Her descendants are there yet. They were the wildest horde of half-naked savages we have found thus far. They swarmed out of mud beehives; out of hovels of the drygoods box pattern; out of gaping caves under shelving rocks; out of crevices in the earth. In five minutes the dead solitude and silence of the place were no more, and a begging, screeching, shouting mob were struggling about the horses' feet and blocking the way. "Bucksheesh! bucksheesh! bucksheesh! howajji, bucksheesh!" It was Magdala over again, only here the glare from the infidel eyes was fierce and full of hate. The population numbers two hundred and fifty, and more than half the citizens live in caves in the rock. Dirt, degradation, and savagery are Endor's specialty. . . . The hill is barren, rocky, and forbidding. No sprig of grass is visible, and only one tree. . . .

Of all the lands there are for dismal scenery, I think Palestine must be the prince. The hills are barren, they are dull of color, they are unpicturesque in shape. The valleys are unsightly deserts fringed with a feeble vegetation that has an expression about it of being sorrowful and despondent. The Dead Sea and the Sea of Galilee sleep in the midst of a vast stretch of hill and plain wherein the eye rests upon no pleasant tint, no striking object, no soft picture dreaming in a purple haze or mottled with the shadows of the clouds. Every outline is harsh, every feature is distinct, there is no perspective—distance works no enchantment here. It is a hopeless, dreary, heart-broken land.

Small shreds and patches of it must be very beautiful in the full flush of spring, however, and all the more beautiful by contrast with the far-reaching desolation that surrounds them on every side. I would like much to see the fringes of the Jordan in spring time, and Shechem, Esdraelon, Ajalon, and the borders of Galilee—but even then these spots would seem mere toy gardens set at wide intervals in the waste of a limitless desolation.

Palestine sits in sackcloth and ashes. Over it broods the spell of a curse that has withered its fields and fettered its energies. Where Sodom and Gomorrah reared their domes and towers, that solemn sea now floods the plain, in whose bitter waters no living thing exists—over whose waveless surface the blistering air hangs motionless and dead—about whose borders nothing grows but weeds, and scattering tufts of cane, and that treacherous fruit that promises refreshment to parching lips, but turns to ashes at the touch. Nazareth is forlorn; about that ford of Jordan where the hosts of Israel entered the Promised Land with songs of rejoicing, one finds only a squalid camp of fantastic Bedouins of the desert. . . . Renowned Jerusalem itself, the stateliest name in history, has lost all its ancient grandeur, and is become a pauper village; the riches of Solomon are no longer there to compel the admiration of visiting Oriental queens; the wonderful temple which was the pride and the glory of Israel is gone. . . .

MY FATHER'S HOUSE

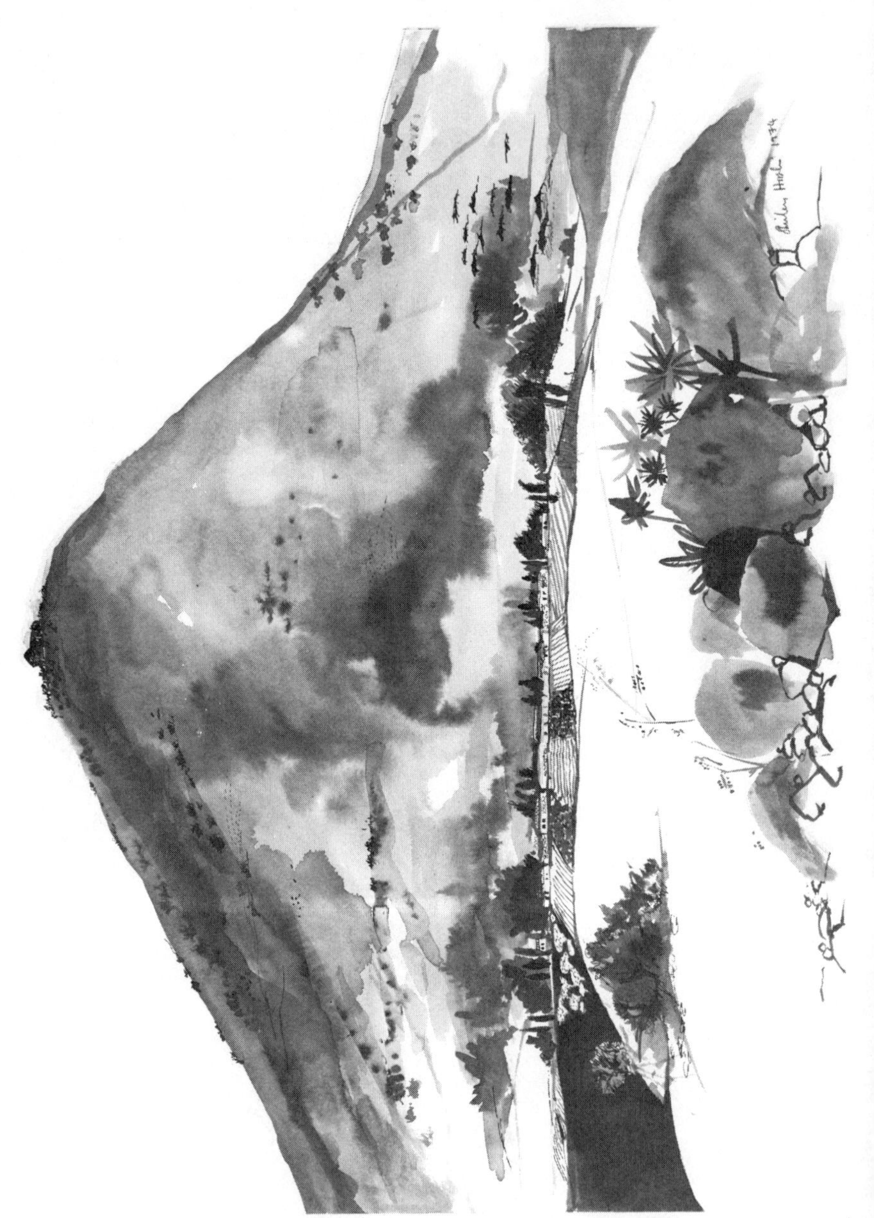

Chapter 1

IN A LITTLE farming village, Kefar Tavor, situated at the foot of the mountain on its most lovely side, the east, I was ushered into the world in October, 1918. The Arab village which preceded it, more like a ruin than a village, had been known by the name of Mascha. That name stuck to the place of my birth. The well-known song by Chaim Chefer, "A Street in Mascha," still moves me every time I hear it, since it bears the name of my village.

In my childhood Kefar Tavor numbered thirty-five families of farmers, some of whom had been born in the country and educated in Rosh-Pina and Zichron-Yaakov; they were joined by several other families including craftsmen, teachers, an unlicensed pharmacist and a doctor. Most of the farmers had come from Romania; a minority were from Russia and Poland, and there was one family from Yemen and another from Mesopotamia. Among the families from Russia were a few converts. My father, who had also come from Russia, was particularly attached to those converts, both as a friend and as a fellow worker.

The farmers were generally blessed with many children. Our family was no exception. My parents brought forth nine offspring, six sons and three daughters; three of them, two girls and a boy, departed from this world as children, before I, the youngest, was born. There remained five brothers and a single sister, who was singular in every respect: Devorah. The difference in age between my eldest brother, Moshe, and myself is twenty-three years.

◈ ◈

Kefar Tavor is situated at the crossroads of the Lower Galilee, in the middle of the plateau. When I was a child, the roads were unpaved. They were no more than narrow dirt tracks that split off in every direction. Transportation was by horse, mule or donkey and also in ox- or mule-drawn wagons. In the summer, trucks might put in an appearance at our village, but only rarely. Their arrival touched off a holiday, and we children used to gather round the self-propelled vehicles, circling them again and again as we tried to fathom the marvelous world they opened up for us. During the rainy season, a time of heavy, engulfing mud, our village was subject to something of a siege. Eventually things were improved with the paving of the Afula road and, later, the roads to Nazareth and Tiberias.

When anyone from the village wanted to go to the big city, a member of his family would drive him by wagon to Afula, where he would take the notoriously slow train through the Jezreel Valley, a section of the Damascus-Haifa line. Arriving in Haifa, he had access to the various conveyances of the time, all of a rather limited efficiency.

Our village was relatively isolated. Its nearest neighbors were Segera, a settlement about eight kilometers to the north, and Yavniel, some ten kilometers to the east. In addition, there were the two little district centers of Tiberias, with its mixed population, some twenty-five kilometers eastward, and Afula, a Hebrew town about eighteen kilometers to the west. Nazareth, in addition to being the marketing center for the Galilee, was the administrative hub of the district; however, Nazareth, which could be foreign and hostile on occasion, was devoid of Jews. Between Kefar Tavor and the other settlements there were Arab villages and Bedouin camps which generally maintained normal, neighborly relations with Kefar Tavor, though this did not discourage many of them from robbing the village's fruit groves and fields, or even stealing an occasional animal from one of the barnyards. In times of emergency, anyone who undertook a journey or a day of work in a remote field did so at the risk of his life.

◈ ◈

The problems of individual and collective security left their mark on every aspect of our lives. When the farmers went out to work, they took their weapons along. These might be licensed hunting rifles, but at times they were illegal pistols concealed beneath their clothes. The entire village was enclosed by a stone wall, fitted with loopholes which could be used for shooting from both standing and kneeling positions. The wall had been formed by connecting the outermost sides of the farm buildings. Twenty meters farther out, a barbed-wire fence was later put up, with adjoining concrete dugouts that served as forward positions.

A good part of the conversation in my parents' home dealt with matters of security. My father, a natural storyteller, had ample opportunity to exercise his talents with tales of his adventures at work and on watch wherever he'd pitched his tent: in Rishon-Letzion, Rosh-Pina, Machanaim, Kefar Tavor and also in the Turkish Army, in which he'd served as a sergeant during the First World War. I was enchanted by the marvelous stories about my eldest brother, Moshe, a man of the world who had been an officer in the Ottoman army, and my brother Mordechai, the second-in-line, who distinguished himself by the courage and resourcefulness he had displayed while serving as one of the four initial watchmen in the village fields; however, the story which moved me the most concerned my brother Zvi (the third), who suffered a stomach wound in a fight against the gang of rustlers from Transjordan that stole our village's cattle in 1920. The story of how Zvi, with two of his buddies, dashed out to intercept the thieves on their way back to Transjordan, shooting it out and charging them, fired my imagination. One of the village boys was killed in that pursuit, Moshe Klimentovski, a relative of ours. Two others, Zvi and Nachman Karniel, were severely wounded but finally recovered. It was said that after he was wounded, my brother asked the Circassian policeman who had rushed to the scene of conflict to lend him his horse. The guardian of the law refused, and thus my brother was obliged to unhorse him. Exhausted and bleeding, Zvi raced the horse home, another bullet hitting him in the side as he galloped straight up to the pharmacy (infirmaries being unknown in those days).

Naturally, I have no personal recollection of the incident—I was two years old at the time—but the story made such an impression on me that I began believing I'd been an eyewitness to it. It happened on the Sabbath which the village had designated as Balfour Declaration Day.* "The village," my sister was to write, "was decorated with greenery and flags; the girls wore white dresses, trimmed with blue ribbons, and blue ribbons also adorned the white shirts of the boys." I've heard the story so often that sometimes it seems I can remember the shouts that rang out in the street: "Cattle thieves!" Zvi

* The Balfour Declaration, an official statement issued on Nov. 2, 1917, by British Foreign Secretary A. J. Balfour, declared that the British government favored "the establishment in Palestine of a national home for the Jewish people."

dashed inside, took the heavy German rifle from where it hung on the wall and ran out to the east, together with his buddies. Papa also took out his Browning pistol from the bottom of the clothes chest in the corner (we had no closet), and together with some other farmers, his neighbors, he hurried to the northern entrance to the village compound to check the Bedouins who, anticipating a Jewish downfall, were trying to break in and plunder the village. Mama went out in front of the house, and my sister, with me in her arms, stood at the window facing the main street. All waited with pounding hearts for news from the front. Suddenly the hoofbeats of a galloping horse were heard and my brother Zvi passed in front of the house, his white shirt now red. He looked back at my mother and yelled: "It's nothing, Mama!" Mama fainted and my ten-year-old sister revived her, with the kind help of our neighbors.

Zvi, having galloped some three kilometers in that condition, had lost a lot of blood. He was "hospitalized" in the pharmacy for a few weeks, till he was out of danger, and only then was he brought home for further treatment. Once he'd regained his strength somewhat, it was possible to transfer him to the real hospital. It took him a full year to recover from his wounds and return to work on the farm.

There were, I repeat, three casualties in the village, one of them dead.

"The day after the raid," my father related afterwards, "the local Arabs wanted to hold a jamboree in the middle of the village, shooting it up and making noise. My house was at the end of the street and there was no one outside at the time. I went out alone and told the merrymakers off: Don't you know what happened yesterday, don't you know about our dead and our wounded? You didn't bother to help us then and now you want to add insult to injury? The wounded men and the women can't stand the rumpus and I'm not going to let you through and whoever tries to break in is going to get shot. Some of them argued that there was no way to get around the village and others grumbled: How can one Jew stop a horde of Moslems? Then some sheiks who knew me stepped forward and told the instigators: We're going to look for another way around, because this Jew is a *Moscovy* (a Russian Jew)—and they retreated." *

⟐ ⟐

Every once in a while, one of the patrolmen from the legendary *Hashomer* † organization would drop in on us, and we were thrilled by the accounts of their marvelous adventures. I was particularly captivated by one of them, Yigael, the hero of the initial settlement of Merchavia and a relative of ours, who was a renowned horseman and story-teller as well. As usual in the world of distant memory, I have a hard time keeping my dates straight, particularly as regards what happened or was told to me when I was very young. I identified so strongly with the tales of our clan that they became a part of myself. Such was the grand story about my father's term of service in the Turkish army. This story, which fits his personality so well, is quoted in my brother's book, *Masechet Shel Bazelet*. Eliav presents it as told by a Mr. Arav, a farmer from Segera who also served with the Turkish forces:

"The Turks wanted to speed up the work on the roads and refused to dismiss the Jews on the High Holy Days of *Rosh-Hashana* and *Yom-Kippur*. Our functionaries in Beer-Sheva tried their best to reverse the decree, but to no avail. Papa decided to act independently, and he informed

* *Fifty Years of Settlement in the Lower Galilee* by Ever Hadani, page 444.

† Self-defense organization of Jewish Pioneers of the Second Aliya, established in Palestine in 1909 to protect the Jewish settlements.

his fellow Jews that if on *Yom-Kippur* all the Jews who worked in the camp would fail to report for work on the grounds that they were sick, he would take the responsibility. Although he was something of a scholar by virtue of his rabbinical studies overseas, Papa wasn't religious in the usual sense of the word; however, he did have a strong national sentiment and great courage.

"Once it was made known to the officer in charge that my father was to blame for the Jews' absence from work on *Yom-Kippur*, he summoned his superior to the camp and Papa was called in to take his punishment. The commandant chose to regard the matter as no less than mutiny, and he sternly asked Papa what he had to say in his defense. Papa didn't lose his self-control; he stood stiffly before the commandant and never lowered his wrathful blue eyes as he fearlessly said: "Sir! I know you are a devout Moslem. Would you have agreed to do hard labor in the desert on one of the holy days of your faith? With us Jews, *Yom-Kippur* is a holy day, and every one of us is ready to lay down his life rather than desecrate it. I admit that I'm responsible for what happened and if you think I deserve it, then punish me and spare my friends. But before you pass judgment I want to appeal to your conscience as a religious man: what I did was right!" Papa's speech and his courageous, forthright stand had their effect on the officer. An hour later he was called in to the commandant again, and the latter said to him: "The punishment for what you did is death by shooting, but I'm going to make allowance for your temperament and forgive you this time."

Another story I loved to hear over and over had to do with an adventure involving Papa, Moshe and Mordechai. It was during the Great War, in the autumn of 1917. Papa's battalion was bivouacking at Uga Al-Chafir on the Sinai border. Moshe was on duty at headquarters in Jerusalem, but then Mordechai was forced into service and ordered to drive a wagon with a pair of mules down to Beer-Sheva. It fell to Mama, Zvi and Eliav to run our farm at Kefar Tavor. Naturally, Papa was worried about how the farm would fare. But it was another concern, the Balfour Declaration which had already been made public, that prompted him to undertake the risky adventure of discharge by desertion.

The Declaration excited my father and aroused hopes in his heart for the advent of our nation's deliverance. He no longer saw any point in serving with the Turkish army, which was fighting Great Britain, a victorious and friendly power. Moshe came to the same conclusion. One day, in the course of duty, he was informed of a plan to move my father's battalion deep into Sinai for a battle with the British. Moshe quickly sent a message to Mordechai to drive his wagon down to Uga Al-Chafir on a certain date. He himself took a few days' leave and raced off on horseback to Uga, through the Hebron mountains and Beer-Sheva. The plan was to liberate Papa and Mordechai from the Turks, whose defeat seemed certain by then. Moshe had connections with the German commandant, and thanks to him Papa was appointed the young officer's servant, in other words his son's. Meanwhile Mordechai arrived at the designated place. In the dark of night my father got on the wagon; the two of them made their way north, to Kefar Tavor, while Moshe returned to his post in Jerusalem. A year later I was born. So it seems that I too am somehow indebted to the Balfour Declaration.

My name, Yigal, was a new one at the time and certainly influenced by the prevailing messianic spirit. The latter was set off by the Balfour Declaration and the wresting of the Land of Israel from Turkish hands by an allied army in which Jews from overseas participated. Thankful parents at the time used the Hebrew root, *gaol*, to express their view of the coming redemption. My father later explained to me how he had chosen my name from the available alternatives, Goel, Yigael and Yigal. *Goel* means redeemer, and my father thought it was too early for that, as I was still an infant. *Yigael* means "He will be redeemed," and my father considered that too passive for his son. Hence he decided on "Yigal," which means "He will redeem."

Moshe was captured by the British and spent two years in a prisoner-of-war camp in Egypt. There he acquired his knowledge of English, having already mastered Arabic, French, German and Turkish. In a word, those were tales of adventure and heroism as told by the people closest to me, my own flesh and blood.

The heroes of those stories were, I repeat, relatives or regular guests in our home. The defense of one's life, property and honor was not an abstract issue but a daily reality. The cultivation of our fields, for example, constantly raised problems of security which made themselves felt every day. My father's three hundred and seventy dunams (a dunam is a quarter of an acre) were divided up, and the several fields were scattered as far as five kilometers from the village. The wagon ride to work at dawn, the lonely spell in the distant fields during the long hours of daylight and the return home in the evening dusk; the night watch over the cut grain that had yet to be gathered in, or was there, in the barn or vineyard; guard duty, assigned to each in his turn over the entire village, outside the wall, to say nothing of the high level of preparedness when tension mounted—such were the matters which concerned me from my earliest childhood, making a deep impression on me and all of us.

◈ ◈

"Whoever wants to conjure up the charm of those places must describe them with topographical accuracy," wrote Konstantin Paustovsky in his book *The Distant Years.*

Kefar Tavor has its own enchanting scenery, its luxuriant vegetation, wild animals and brilliant birds. In the center of it all, Mount Tabor soars like a giant dome. It's a beautiful mountain, the most beautiful I've ever seen. "Maybe there are others more beautiful, but none is just as beautiful," if I might be permitted to paraphrase a line from one of Natan Alterman's poems. I regard it that way even now, though I've seen mountains that surpass it in size and height. It stands apart among the surrounding mountains, a firm, burly loner with distinctive features all its own and a magnificent summit. Dark carpets are spread at its foot, broad strips of very fertile soil.

The mountain displays a wide variety of plant life: oak trees, terebinths, birches, pines and jujubes cover a considerable part of its steep slopes. It possesses a wealth of vistas and colors, whose changes reflect the passing hours of day and the seasons of the year. At its top are the church buildings which fit in well with the architectural scheme of Nature, though if I may say so they always seemed like strangers to me whenever I attained the mountain's broad summit.

Coming to the mountain and wandering about the monasteries on top, I had the feeling I was in another land.

When I was studying at the Kaduri agricultural school, we used to climb the mountain as a group, stopping at the church and strolling through the narrow, stone passageway between the two main courtyards. Sometimes I'd come across a pretty nun, and the combination of chastity and beauty rested heavily on the mind. Occasionally there would be an exchange of glances, but they would be averted quickly enough. Such a glance would sometimes stay with me for days. More than once I went back there, secretly hoping to come across the young nun with the pale face and lovely eyes, but I never saw her again.

I had a powerful love for the smells of my native village.

The smells of the house, the yard, the animals; the smell of manure and the smell of the plowed, harvested, dry fields; the smell of the almond trees, the wild flowers, the greenery, and above all the smell of the earth after the first rain. The hay's fragrance was another term for the smells of love.

Some of the wild plants were actually useful to us. With the thorny jujube branches we'd erect fences for the grain shed or the small vegetable garden. The burnet bushes made good brooms for sweeping out the yard; we also used them as a protective covering for the little sprouts in the tobacco nursery. The opuntia hedges, in addition to serving as natural barriers for the defense of our orchards, offered us sweet, juicy fruit in their season. There was a wild fruit known by its Arab name, *akub*, with which we regularly stuffed our lamb roasts, producing a delicacy fit for a king. Green mallow leaves were used in the preparation of dishes that were unforgettably aromatic and tasty. And no less cherished were the sorrel leaves, an added spice to our green salads which were flavored with olive oil, lemon juice, salt and pepper. The soft stalks of the fennel are also fondly remembered, as well as the *sinaryah*, the *chorfesh* and the bitter *murar*. We used to pick *murar* stems in the field, peel them in order to take away some of their bitterness and chew them to our hearts' content. On hot summer days we'd eat jujubes by the mouthful, little berries rich in content with an intoxicating smell. All along Wadi Midi, thorny raspberry bushes grew wild. Their tart fruit was good to taste but not always easy to digest. As a country boy, I had little trouble distinguishing between poisonous and edible mushrooms. Picking them was one of my favorite pastimes, as was eating them, boiled or fried. A special springtime treat was the mandrake, small, orange apples with a heady fragrance, very tasty when fully ripe. There were many legends concerning the mandrake. More than once I heard about its medicinal and aphrodisiac properties from the Arab farmers. The fact that this matter was brought up in the Bible as well led me to believe them all the more. It was only natural that in our youth we had a craving for those miraculous little apples.

While we're on the subject of delicacies, something must be said about hunting. For as long as my mother lived, we never dared bring any game into the house, since she kept a kosher kitchen. It was otherwise after her demise, when hares, partridges, wild pigeons, starlings and, less frequently, a flank of deer would find their way to our table. They were not only hunted with a rifle but also with primitive traps, which our neighbors taught us how to make.

Chapter 2

I'VE ALREADY mentioned Wadi Midi. Now is the time to enlarge upon the system of wadis—streams that are dry except in the rainy season—which dissect the plateau of the Lower Galilee about Kefar Tavor. They were not only a prominent feature of the countryside, but also unforgettable scenes of childhood.

Three main wadis flow, in the winter, from north to south, and another one, the biggest, from west to east: the farthest west is Wadi Midi, which drains the rain water from the eastern slopes of the Nazareth range and Mount Tabor; we had always suffered from a shortage of water for irrigation and sometimes even for drinking, and that was why we were so thrilled, especially as children, to see the mass of water flowing there in the winter. On not a few rainy days we risked our health and possibly our lives as well by undressing—so long as our group was composed solely of boys, of course—and taking a dip in the rushing, muddy stream.

At one end of that wadi, near its source, on the road from Kefar Tavor to Segera (opposite what is now the entrance to Bet-Keshet), there arose from among the rocks, as if it had grown out of them, an ancient, spacious building known as Suk Al-Khan, a cross between a fortress and a hostel for man and his animals. In the days of the Turks, that ancient stronghold served as a stopping place for the caravans journeying by camel, mule or donkey from Damascus to Jerusalem, or to Yafo and the coastal plain on the way to Gaza and Egypt. Opposite the khan to the west of the road was a more ancient site, from the Second Temple Period according to some, a smaller version of the khan which had served the same purpose in its day. Evidently the historic routes didn't change very much in the course of time. But whereas those sites had afforded security to the travelers of antiquity, in my childhood they gave rise to fear and dread. In their deserted ruins, made of gray limestone which had blackened with age, gangs of bandits used to hide out. There was something mysterious, alternately appealing and repulsive, about the cracked walls and the gaping watchtowers. Admission to the stronghold's court was at the price of uneasiness, not to mention fear. Yet my curiosity and hopes of discovering something ancient and unknown among the ruins, or possibly the simple urge for adventure, helped me to overcome my boyish fears.

The easternmost wadi is named Shumar for its abundant growth of wild fennel (*shamir* in Hebrew). This wadi is farther away from the village, an unruly thicket to the eye. From its steep slopes, we used to pluck the wild fennel stalks out of which we fashioned the roofs of our tabernacles for the feast of that name. We also used to hunt partridges there, and pursue rabbits and gazelles. That was also the wadi where my brother Zvi was wounded, as I've related. No wonder I felt a mysterious bond drawing me to it; as I moved through its passages I was filled with fear, curiosity and pride. East of the village, between those two wadis and parallel to them ran gorgeous Wadi Mascha, which we regarded as second to none, the most interesting of our wadis.

This was due first of all to the ruins which stand on one

of its banks, those of the ancient site of Mascha which had been referred to as Shachtsimah in Egyptian papyri. Actually, we never succeeded in solving the puzzle of Mascha's name. All we knew was that its ruins encompassed the grave of a Moslem holy man, a dervish by the name of Al-Maschawi. The grave was held sacred by the Arabs of the Galilee, who flocked there to prostrate themselves on its stones. A legend circulated among the local Arabs about two does which used to visit the holy grave every night; the dervish would milk them, and he had their milk to thank for his eternal life. Interestingly enough, I never talked to an Arab about the legend without his believing it implicitly. Yet none of them knew if Mascha had been named after the dervish, or if it was the other way round. The ruins of ancient Mascha also offered a steady supply of shards, ancient coins and other trinkets, mute reminders of the life that had gone on there in distant days. It was also the site of dark, mysterious caves which simultaneously attracted and repelled us.

Secondly, this wadi abounds in vivid wild flowers, ranging from the anemone and cyclamen to the blue lupine.

Thirdly, there was a cemetery on its bank in which the village founders were laid to rest. In one of the graves slept my mother, Chayah-Etil, who had passed away in the prime of her life, when I was still a little boy. Moreover, there was a bubbling spring in the wadi from which we used to draw our water. Wadi Mascha was less wild than its neighbors, and a considerable part of its steep banks was cultivated. Near one of its cliffs stood a small but thick grove of eucalyptus trees which was an ideal spot for our children's games; during heat waves we used to rest in its cool shade. Not far from the spring was the village flour mill, which stood idle most of the year owing to mechanical failures. When the mill went out of commission we had our wheat ground in Kefar Kama, the neighboring Circassian village that contained two flour mills which somehow remained in operation at all times. We used to take a sack or two of wheat over there by wagon or mule-back, pour their contents into the big funnel on one side of the mill and receive our flour on the other side, at the end of the grinding line. Those mills could process anything—wheat, corn, legumes—each according to its needs and crops.

The trip to the flour mill and the meetings with other villagers, Jews, Arabs and Circassians, filled us with a holiday spirit, a feeling quite different from that which prevailed on the arduous days of work or during our school term. I remember that while waiting for my turn I sometimes strolled around the narrow alleyways of the Circassian village, taking it all in, stopping at a stall and buying myself some *rachatlakum* and homemade candy which were unique in taste and brilliant color. Occasionally I would go to a store and fit myself out with a new whip or some other piece of riding equipment. More than once, I would brave the very real danger of the male inhabitants' merciless jealousy and steal a glance at a glance directed my way, at the stranger, from behind the veils of the lovely Circassian girls. It was another world, foreign and enchanting.

But we must return to Wadi Mascha. The wadi contained, as I mentioned, a spring which was the source of our drinking water. The mouth of the well was enclosed by hewn stones. Since there was no pump available, the farmers used to make the journey to the spring twice a week with their barrel-laden wagons. The job of letting the bucket down to the depths of the spring's clear water was reserved for my father or my brother Eliav (number four) and unfortunately withheld from me, the baby. My task was to take the overflowing bucket from them and

empty it into a barrel. When the barrels were full, we covered them with well-washed sacks, using iron hoops to tighten them about the barrel's mouth. In about half an hour's time, the wagon would be creeping up the steep bank of the wadi (a formidable problem in itself!) toward our yard. There, empty barrels stood in a row, and the fresh water was promptly poured into them by the previous method, in order to free the wagon for its numerous other duties. It was only in the thirties that a water pump was installed north of the village, the pump which supplies the village's drinking water to this very day.

I've been lavish with my praise for Wadi Mascha; however, the king of the wadis, the deepest and most interesting of all, is Nachal Tavor, or as we called it then, by its Arab name, Wadi Sharar. Its source is on the watershed southwest of Mount Tavor (one of the tributaries of the Kishon runs in the opposite direction). It flows from west to east, and it not only has sources of its own but collects additional water from the abovementioned wadis. It also flows more constantly than the others. Nachal Tavor runs down to Wadi Bira (apparently the Biblical Beth-barah) which heads for the Jordan and drops into it south of Naharaim. That's also the site of the ruined Crusader fortress, a mysterious stronghold which the Arabs called Kaukav Al-Hava and whose present name is Kochav-Hayarden (Jordan Star). Reaching it, we would look out, entranced, at the bare, wild landscape of the mountains of Gilead soaring across the way, and at the broad, deep valley that divided us from them. The powerful, shrieking winds which buffeted the fortress even in the middle of summer lent a breathtaking air of former majesty to the place.

Legends circulated about that wadi and tales of banditry were ascribed to it. The truth was that it served as an entry for the gangs of thieves and smugglers who infiltrated from Transjordan; from there the bandits darted forth and under the cover of its winding slopes they made off with their booty. Whenever there was a drought in Transjordan, the wadi would be teeming with nomads who would spread out and raid the property of the Jewish and Arab farmers on this side of the Jordan. A hike in that wadi was always regarded as a special treat, which included the anxious anticipation of unexpected events. Maybe that was actually the reason for our frequent visits there. However, it was only on rare occasions that we dared to push on through it to the Jordan. Whenever I happened to be there I stood and gazed in astonishment at the jutting, mysterious cliffs. I was sure that somewhere near its end there was a secret passage to the ends of the earth.

I developed a strong attachment to the scenes of my childhood. I used to tour the surrounding area frequently, either on foot or mounted, first on a donkey and later a mare, my own; sometimes with a group but usually alone. I went on many school trips with my teachers for guides, they being extremely well-versed in the history of Israel and its flora and fauna. Pages from the Bible and the history of the Zealots, the Crusaders and the Islamic period became a reality of buildings, earth and stone as we wandered about the sites which had been mentioned in the chronicles of the land.

The Bible stories added a new dimension to my jaunts on Mount Tabor, which had been familiar to me from the time I first opened my eyes. True, it was no less real than before. The same church buildings towered at its summit, foreigners to me. However, as I climbed it now the exploits of Deborah and Barak were re-enacted before my eyes; here, I would say to myself, was where the ten thousand from the tribe of Naphtali and the tribe of Zebulun had stood. As I rambled by the Kishon River I recalled the story of Sisera and Jael, the wife of Heber the Kenite, as well as that of the city of Hazor in the Upper Galilee. Without being schooled in strategy I couldn't help remarking, even then, the wisdom Barak had displayed in maneuvering Sisera's forces with their chariots of iron toward the swamps on the banks of the Kishon. I admired Barak and when I happened to receive the part of Sisera in one of our school plays, I had a hard time coming to terms with it.

Trips to the Gilboa and its vicinity gave me a glimpse of the lives, the noble courage and the death of Saul and Jonathan, and to complete the tragic picture my window at home looked out on the Arab village of En-dor, where I remembered King Saul, whom I considered the saddest and most beloved of Israel's kings. On more than one occasion, we quietly scouted around En-dor for a trace of the witch's hut. The spirit of Saul, my king, hovered over the place. One day a visiting lecturer appeared in our village, Shaul Tschernikhovski, my favorite poet, who also served a brief term as our country doctor. His firm stance, his face, his mustache and flowing hair enchanted me. I too went to hear his lecture on Saul (Shaul in Hebrew), David and Jonathan. I was a child and couldn't remember everything he said, of course, but I remember the gist of it, particularly the comparison he drew between the characters of Saul and David.

"Just think," said Saul the poet, "how great King Saul must have been. Our history was written by David's henchmen, but even they weren't able to diminish his stature. And if that was their image of him, it's easy to imagine how great a man he really was."

The poet won my sympathy and gave expression to my own feelings. I had always wavered between the heroic figure of David, the sweet singer of Israel, and the more modest one of Saul, and my heart went out not to David but to Saul, the man who had gone to look for his father's donkeys and found a kingdom. The child in me refused to accept David's flight to the Philistine camp; I believed that no matter how great a danger one was in, there could be no thought of seeking refuge in the enemy camp. And the Philistines were the enemies of Israel, not just Saul's personal enemies. Neither did I believe that the lamentation David had composed for Saul and Jonathan was sincere; it seemed artificial, designed to achieve some practical gain, and hence his lament for Saul, his rival for the royal crown, didn't carry conviction. The strange circumstances of Abner's murder at the hands of Joab, David's commander-in-chief, also raised doubts in my mind. True, David proclaimed his disavowal of the murder, but I had a lingering suspicion that Joab had acted on David's behalf, since if it were otherwise, I asked myself, why didn't David punish him? The episode concerning Absalom also gave cause for thought, but the straw that broke the camel's back was the assigning of Uriah the Hittite, the faithful, devoted officer, to the place where the fighting was hardest so that he should fall there, giving David a free hand with his beautiful wife. All this was carried out by Joab, David's confidant and minister, and I couldn't forgive either one of them. I had to take comfort in the courage of Nathan the prophet, with his pronouncement regarding the poor man's lamb. More than once I said to myself that if God had decreed that David, the nation's idol, shouldn't build the temple, it wasn't because of his wars against his enemies but on account of his deeds within his own camp. I admired David for what he did to Goliath, and for his psalms and valor, but I abhorred his abominations. After hearing Shaul Tschernikhovski I had no further doubts about the matter, and the modest figure of King Saul grew taller all the more.

Even Samuel, who had deserted Saul, aroused my resentment. After the lecture, on my way home, I told Papa what I've said here. Papa's response was a lingering kiss on my brow, with my head in his two strong hands.

The childhood scenes I've described were simple and familiar, scenes that could be viewed and traveled and touched, but under the influence of the tales connected with them, they gained in significance. So it was with Nachal Harod and Beth-barah, the battlefields of Gideon, whom I preferred among the Judges. So also with the Safed area, which I could no longer consider without reflecting on Shimeon Bar-Yochai, the pious sage who was forced into hiding, and Yochanan from Gush-Chalav, the Galilean hero who thrashed the Romans, and his antithesis, Yosef Ben-Mattityahu (Flavius) whom I, the country boy, pictured as an aristocratic Jerusalemite who had not only failed as a military commander but also betrayed his fellow soldiers in the Galilean fortress of Jotapata. This may sound odd, but the fact that his betrayal took place in the Galilee somehow turned that distant event into a decidedly personal affair. It was not only a matter of scenery but of events that occurred on Galilean soil, in the distant or more recent past. How moved I was, at once thrilled and respectful, as I peered into the Zealots' caves about the Arbel! It was the same with Bet-Shan, with the historical connotations it held for me, as well as Tsipori, Akko's walls, Safed, Tiberias and, above all, the Horns of Hattin, which had witnessed the decisive battle between the Islamic armies and the Crusaders, and Tel-Chai,* about whose heroic stand and fall I knew well from the stories of the *Hashomer* patrolmen who visited our home.

I regarded the Tel-Chai episode with mixed feelings; on the one hand my sympathy was aroused by the terrible loneliness of the valiant few who determined to stand their ground in that remote spot with its hostile surroundings, in the face of grave dangers, with no one but themselves to count on; but on the other hand I couldn't overlook Papa's stern criticism of Trumpeldor, for the mistake he'd made in opening the gate and allowing the armed Arabs of

* The isolated Jewish settlement in the Upper Galilae, established in 1918 as a camp for shepherds. It was razed by the Arabs in 1920.

Chalsa in to search for the Frenchmen who were supposed to be hidden there. "He was a hero," Papa used to say, "but he acted like a recruit. He just didn't know how cunning his neighbors could be."

Even Christian Nazareth and the campaigns of the Crusaders and their Moslem adversaries stirred my imagination, since they were associated with fortresses that towered on the land I saw as my own. My sense of identification with the Galilee and my Galilean home, the place of my birth, was by no means entirely due to the tutelage of my father and teachers. It came to me naturally. And although I knew my nation's history, I felt as if I'd never been exiled from the land and my father hadn't returned to it from Russia. My roots were here, in the rocky Galilean soil.

Chapter 3

MY PERSONAL STORY is entitled *My Father's House*, but to tell the truth it should have been *my father's and mother's*, not only to maintain formal equality between the sexes or to honor both father and mother, but because they both left their mark on the story of my parental home and gave it form and direction. Now I shall try to describe that home, as I remember it.

Our house stood in the higher part of the village, near the northern entrance. It faced the main street, to the east, and our yard was in back, to the west. About the yard, like an enclosure, stood the farm buildings: a henhouse for a few hundred fowl; a stable containing a pair of mules and a yoke of oxen (which were later replaced by another pair of mules), a mare and a donkey; a barn that numbered some twenty head of cattle—we called them "tails" on account of their meager yields—mostly of local stock with a minority of the Damascus breed, which were fed on natural pasture with an extra portion of fodder from our fields. We also raised a few goats. Next to the yard's western wall was our *tabun*, an Arab oven buried in the ground whose fuel, coarse straw, was flameless and maintained a steady temperature. The stove itself was made out of fired claq with fragments of pottery scattered at the bottom to retain the heat. Its round opening had an iron cover with a

handle, and once a day, usually toward evening, we would remove the ashes and throw in fresh straw. That was the stove in which my mother, and after her death my sister, baked the best bread I ever tasted. It was also used for preparing dishes which required slow cooking. The *tabun*'s smell clung to the village of my birth. It drifted through the yards and was twice as sharp on hot days and evenings, when there was no wind to set the air in motion. On such days that heavy, unique smell would enfold the houses and the sky above them.

In a more distant corner of the yard stood the outhouse, whose floor boards were placed over a deep hole. Though we tried our best to keep it clean, it was hardly sanitary.

Since, as I've said, we had no running water, there was no point in building a shower. But we did have to wash ourselves, at least once a week and even more often during the sweaty seasons. Such a bath was quite an undertaking. We would boil a big pot of water and pour half of it into a bucket, adding cold water so that it wouldn't be too hot; then we would stand naked in a washtub and use a cup to pour the water over our heads and bodies, soaping ourselves and finally rinsing with the cup. In time, one of the farmers came up with an ingenious invention, which didn't simplify things any. He erected a wooden frame which held a barrel with a faucet on the bottom; the frame was enclosed by a "shower curtain" of sacks. Hot and cold water were poured into the barrel, a fine example of progress which nevertheless demanded more labor than the former method.

Another building was designed as a granary, with wooden bins lined with galvanized sheet metal. There we stored the grain for home and animal consumption till the next harvest ripened; it was also the place where we stored the seeds that were to be planted for the next year's crop. When the time came for storing away the new crop it was I, the skinny tot, who would slip through the bin's swinging gate and sweep out the old grain which remained at the bottom, while my father said: "You shall clean out the old to make way for the new."

In the middle of the yard stood the wagon. It was made entirely of fine wood, including its four wheels whose rims were of thick steel. Extending from its front end were wooden shafts reinforced with iron bands, their length that of the draft animals; they had a stabilized base and chains at the tip for harnessing the mules. In the plowing and seeding seasons, the winter and spring, the wagon assumed the shape of an oblong box whose sides were easily removed and reassembled. In harvest time the boards were replaced by hayracks and tall, wooden poles to bring in the crops. In another corner of the yard stood the shed where our equipment was stored: plows for single animals and pairs, harrows, cultivators and so on.

There were two gates to the yard: the one facing the street was wide and high while the other, more like a wicket, was set right in the wall and led out to the garden, the grain shed and the manure heap behind the yard. In front of the house there was a garden enclosed by a fence where we raised fruit trees and other ornamental varieties, as well as vegetables and a few beds of flowers.

In another corner of the yard stood the hut belonging to the *charat*, the Arab tenant farmer. There he lived with his wife and children, who cooperated in the farm work in exchange for a share of the crops.

The house itself was of local limestone construction, with a large cellar; its roof was of red Marseilles tiles, a product of the rural French architectural style whose influence extended to us through Baron Rothschild's enterprises. Though the house was definitely not small in size, one could hardly approve of the way its interior was laid out. All in all there were two big rooms, one of which served as a kitchen, dining room and an extra place to sleep, and the other as both parlor and bedroom.

In a corner of the kitchen stood a round metal bin, painted dark red, which contained the ground flour. Above it hung round sieves with pliant wooden sides and meshes fashioned from narrow strips of leather; the size of their openings varied in proportion to the grains that were to be sifted in the grain shed. One small, delicate sifter was designed to separate the bran from the flour. A woven straw tray (*tabak* in Arabic) also hung on the wall as a decoration, and when necessary it was used as an accessory for baking or serving the meals. Even now I can't understand how we got along with only two rooms. However, I don't remember that we ever complained about the house being too small.

Actually, most of the year we didn't sleep inside at all. Some of us would pass the night in the grain shed or the hut in our vineyard—a combination of rest and guard duty—and the others on a wooden board which my father would put down in the yard every summer, next to the wall of the house. On that board the housewife would spread mats, sheets and mattresses, and all of us, except for our parents, who slept inside, would pass the night there one beside the other, enjoying the starry summer sky overhead and the cool evening wind that blew across the broad fields. It was wonderful to lie there and listen to the sounds of the stirring night outdoors and look at the full or crescent moon. We would be awakened by the fresh, dewy touch of the dawn. Sleeping together beneath the open sky was a special summer treat for us, to which we looked forward again when winter came with its wind and rain.

Sleeping outdoors also involved not a little danger. One morning when I was about four years old, I rose from my outdoor bed and when my mother went to collect the bedding she discovered, beneath my pillow, a coiled viper sleeping peacefully away. She let out a hair-raising scream and immediately fainted. The snake tried to flee but a blow from my father's stick, crushed its head. Mama rushed to the synagogue bearing a batch of candles and an offering of oil for the eternal light, and uttering the Benediction of Deliverance and a prayer of thanksgiving to the Creator of the World for having saved me.

The uninvited company of snakes—those long, creeping sticks, as the children called them—troubled us almost every summer. My father became a real expert at hunting them down. Discovering them at a distance, he would shoot at them with his hunting rifle and never miss; encountering them at close range, he would crush them with a stick, pitchfork or stone. I remember once a snake was sighted in our kitchen. My father shut the door to cut off its route of escape and began chasing it with his stick. He ordered me to climb onto the table and follow the snake's movements. The battle was alternately frightful and heartwarming. In a moment of despair the snake straightened up on its tail and sprang at my father. I caught my breath, but Papa, moving aside, spun around and with a swift blow of his stick hit the snake, which made a final effort and took refuge in a large jar of water. My father quickly closed the jar and with that the battle was over. Even my sister Dèvorah once took hold of a snake instead of a bunch of grapes during the grape-picking season, and miraculously her hand wasn't bitten. My brother Eliav kept pet canaries in a cage. The cage hung at the front of the house, and one day when he climbed up to it to feed his birds a viper sprang out at him. Fortunately, the snake's feathered prey had caused its belly to swell, and thus it remained stuck between the bars of the cage where it met its end at the hands of my father.

My green-eyed cat also became known as a first-rate snake fighter, in addition to her fame as a hunter of mice. One blazing summer day, around sundown, I with my father breathlessly followed the course of the battle she waged against a big, dangerous viper. The repulsive snake, with its short body and tail, kept swinging its triangular head, with its brown and orange spots, waving it from side to side as it relentlessly followed the cat's movements. The event took place in one of the corners of the yard, by a pile of stones which had apparently served the snake as a hiding place. Now as well it had apparently been willing to withdraw to its refuge, but my cat blocked its route of escape. Like a trained boxer, she protected her face with one paw while using the other to land a blow on the snake's head. Suddenly the snake reared up to half its height and tried to strike the cat's nose with lightning speed, but she, astoundingly agile, dodged the snake by shifting her head to the opposite side, and with an unexpected blow her paw slammed down on its neck and stunned it at once. A few additional blows and the battle was decided. Very quietly, as if nothing had happened, she removed herself from the scene of conflict.

A valiant fighter, she could also be innocent and friendly. As cats will, she frequently chose my bed as a good place to rest, and when sleeping she would snore slightly, in a soothing rhythm. And the innocent kitty knew how to scratch too, whenever she was in heat, desperate with love. So it was that in the winter evenings, especially during the month of *Shevat*, the yards and porches were transformed into scenes of feline passion. It was hard to catch the cats in the act, but one could easily follow what was going on by the sounds that rent the stillness of the night. The full-grown males banded about their shapely opposite members and serenaded them with wails of love, rising and falling in rhythm. Once actual contact was made, the tomcats' howls became fiercer and more prolonged, leaping by octaves from a pleading, seductive wail to a wild roar which terminated in high cries of satisfaction. The puzzle was why the cat's wail became a heartbreaking scream just as he reached the peak of sexual gratification, and this was an unfailing source of jokes and folk tales, with countless variations. A common rebuke for grumblers without cause in our village was "Stop howling like a cat in winter!"

I acquired my cat after the death of my dog, Navchan. A boy my age, the son of Sheik Otman, who was the tough chief of the A-Zabiach Bedouin tribe, made me a gift of him while he was still a tender pup. He was light-colored, between white and grey, and even though he was of ordinary local stock, without any glorious pedigree, he was marvelously handsome. We became attached to one another in a bond of loyalty and great affection. He accompanied me on my many jaunts on foot and horseback; he guarded the yard against thieves and would bound towards me as I returned from school or a game in the town council square. Everyone in my family was attached to him. One day Papa said to me: "Son, you're going to have to part with Navchan. I know he's very nice, but it's better to raise a cat than a dog. We don't need a watchdog; after all, we have watchmen in the village, but we do need someone who can fight off all those snakes. That's a job for a cat. And it's hard to raise a cat and a dog in the same place—very hard, you might say. So there's no alternative: we have to give him away to someone who lives far from here."

None of Papa's arguments had any effect. I refused to part with Navchan.

Navchan was marvelously handsome, much in demand among the female dogs of the village; however, in the long run he paid for his sex appeal with his life. This is the way it happened: one Sunday while I was at school, a British police officer from Nazareth arrived in our village, bringing with him a trained pedigreed hunting dog, a female, and in heat. The officer had come on a hunting trip through the surrounding fields and ravines, but before taking to the fields he went over to Frieda Goldman's inn for a bite to eat. His aristocratic, pedigreed bitch remained in the street. Emerging, he saw the noble bitch making love with a common native dog. He tried to separate them, but to no avail. They spun around in a ring, stuck together in typical canine passion. In order to avenge this insult to the lauded British empire, he shot Navchan in the head and killed him on the spot. The innkeeper told me that even after the murder the dogs refused to be parted, and the imperial officer was obliged, with his own two hands, to uncouple his bitch from her despicable, slain lover as she let out heartbreaking wails.

For a long time I refused to be comforted. I laid my dog to rest with honor near the outer wall of our yard. Now there was no obstacle and my father could bring us the kitten. In her battles with the snakes, as I've described, she revealed exceptional courage. Even today, though many years have passed, I can clearly remember her flashing eyes, flaming in the dark like two green lamps.

In the parlor, which also served as the master bedroom, there was a big chest that took the place of a clothes closet. An antique clock stood elegantly at the middle of one wall, chiming every half hour. Another wall was decorated with a large mirror in a carved wooden frame; as adolescents we used it to examine our hair, combing it into that uncombed look which was the height of fashion in those days. The big, rectangular table, my father's handiwork, stood at the center of the enormous room. My finest memories are tied in with that table: it was where we used to sit on our holiday evenings, the big family assembled about it, and it was where our many guests dined, having stopped off for a night in our home; together with us it mutely listened to the gripping stories they brought with them from all over the country and world. The furniture was modest and functional, but not owing to any lack of funds. The walls were bare, without pictures. A few books were scattered here and there, and on the little cupboard, from within glass-covered frames, a host of family photographs looked out at us. In the evenings, sooty kerosene lamps waged the war of light against the surrounding darkness. The lamps produced a unique, rather mysterious light, which flickered at every infiltration of the wind.

In one corner and another stood the *jarot*, the polymorphic water jars which the Arab peddlers used to bring around every spring, wrapped in woven rope nets. It was a wonder to us that they never got broken during their long ride on the animal's back. Arriving in the village, the peddlers spread out straw mats, removed the jars from their nets and advertised their wares in loud, warbling voices. The clay jars were our substitute for ice, which was nowhere to be found, and took the place of the refrigerator, of which we had never even heard. On blazing summer days we were grateful to them for having chilled the water or kept the fruits and vegetables fresh. Next to the jars stood the clay pots which were employed in our cheese industry. The jars were works of art in themselves: black as basalt or fair as limestone, some of them tall and wasp-waisted, bearing a remarkable resemblance to the Arab girls with thir bodies held straight as they carried water jars on their heads, without their hands touching them, and others with big bellies, bringing pregnant women to mind. Like children, so to speak, the smaller jars stood among them with a narrow spout on their sides, they being the drinking vessels. Every spring my father would buy me my own private drinking jar which I used to take with me when going out to the grain shed or vineyard. I well remember the way I practiced drinking till I learned to use the jar properly, in the Arab fashion, which was to hold it an arm's length above the mouth and sip the thin trickle without the spout touching your lips.

Once every two years we replaced our old baskets with new ones, they too purchased from the Arab peddlers. The baskets were made out of woven rushes. Like the jars, the baskets were of various dimensions: big ones for carrying the eggs which were to be bought by Masud the trader; medium-sized baskets for purchases or lunch when working the whole day in the fields; little baskets for the children's meals in school or on trips.

Our farm was based on nonirrigated crops. We followed a biennial cycle of crop rotation: half our fields were set aside for winter crops and the other half for summer crops. The first half contained the cereals, wheat and barley—the *chasid;* the second, legumes or corn and sorghum—the *karab*. The fields which had been in *karab* the previous year were sown the next year with *chasid* crops, and vice versa. That was our version of biennial crop rotation. Hence there was always something to be harvested, gathered and taken to market. We also had a vineyard for wine grapes and an almond grove, which were each twenty dunams in size. In the case of Galilean farms, such crops had no need of supplementary irrigation, and their chief advantage was that they didn't have to be marketed every day. A considerable part of our requirements for home consumption came from our farm, first and foremost being the bread we ate, which we baked as loaves or in the Arab style. We had plenty of eggs, but we never ate much chicken. The barn supplied us with milk and its products, butter, cream, cheese and buttermilk, as well as the curds which we used to preserve in large glass jars, soaked in olive oil. Since at the time there were no separators available, we used to pour the milk into black clay jars, and within a few days the cream would be floating on top with the sour milk underneath. Then we used to collect the cream in a goatskin, shaking it right and left and up and down to form a solid whitish-yellow mass of butter. In time, we acquired a simple, hand-operated churn. The sour milk we either drank with pleasure or used as a raw material in the manufacture of salty Safed cheese. With the aid of special pills, we speeded up the coagulation of the milk. When it had coagulated sufficiently, we emptied it into woven baskets made out of split rushes; the liquid would drip out and in a few days cheese would form in the shape of a big, thick disc marked with the grooves of the rushes.

And of course there were seasonal dishes, or those which were prepared in a specific season. Grapes, wine grapes in particular, were never absent from our table when in season, till we were fairly glutted with them. Towards the end of the grape-picking season our home would be pervaded by an intoxicating, bittersweet smell, that of the jam boiling in giant vats of galvanized copper; I liked to stand by those vats as my sister stirred them with a long wooden spoon and watch the Alicante and Bordeaux grapes as they burst and melted in the heat of the fire below. Once the cooking stage was over, the jam would be poured from the giant vats into big glass jars, where it was stored till the next grape-picking season.

The Alicante and Bordeaux jam would adorn our table several times a day, whereas the aristocratic Muscatel jam, in which the fruit retained its fullness, was served on the Sabbaths and holidays and occasionally on an ordinary weekday, if we happened to have guests. My sister was forced to contend with Eliav in a battle of hideouts waged with much ingenuity and resourcefulness, seeing that he with his sweet tooth had developed a particular affection for Muscatel jam. In no time at all he could polish off a quantity of jam that was meant to last a few days, not to mention seasons.

Next to the house we kept a little vegetable garden, but aside from onions, cucumbers, radishes and little patches of parsley, pungent reseda and fragrant peppermint, we grew no vegetables, simply because we were short of water; however, there were plenty of vegetables to be had at home. They were transported on mule-back by Arab peddlers coming from Bikat Bet-Netofa, which had water to spare. And in season there were, of course, the almonds which we waited for longingly, and the green chickpeas which we ate with relish whether fresh or baked; so it was with the corn, which was delicious whether boiled or browned on the fire. There was a special flavor to the young grape leaves when they were stuffed with rice and meat. The food was natural and simple, the fruit of land and labor which were ours.

Chapter 4

WE USED the Hebrew calendar which revolved about the Sabbaths and holidays, its glory. However, our daily lives followed a different calendar, that of the seasons of the year and its transformations. The feeling of autumn in the village was not restricted to that wonderful, brief passage from the heat waves to other days, and particularly nights, which were cooler; our rural autumn meant the removal of the summer crops from the shed to the granary, while corn cobs and sorghum were to be gathered into the shed. With the coming of autumn the fields of stubble came in for a deep plowing with the moldboard plow till the *karab* was well turned over—in other words the fields from which the fertilizing legumes had been gathered, so as to keep up the crop rotation by sowing cereals. In autumn the first *chatsav* flowers broke out of the ground. They did so under their own power, so to speak, without the aid of heaven and its rain. Anxiously, we waited for the first rain, and its arrival gladdened the eyes and heart. Autumn brought the great holidays, *Rosh-Hashana* and *Yom-Kippur*, whose fast was strictly observed by the entire population of the village, without exception. When I was a boy I made do, like most of the village children, with a half-day's fast. Then there was the Feast of Tabernacles, whose building and decorating put us in a festive mood, and the most cheerful of all were us, the children.

On holidays, the children of the village who had grown up and gone off to take root in other fields came back home. Naturally, some of them had emigrated to the city to set themselves up in some office job, as people would even then. But most of them had left in order to establish new farming villages. The holiday gathering of the entire Mascha clan added to the sense of festivity and gave us a feeling of strength and affiliation. The festive dinner on the eve of the holiday, the stories about what was going on in the new villages which had just been founded, the gifts, the friendly expressions—such were the things which separated those evenings from the usual chain of events. When it was time for the Reading of the Torah the next morning, all the children of pre-Bar Mitzvah age would be assembled in the synagogue where they were draped in large prayer shawls, and it was the children who would recite the blessing in unison in a loud, merry voice. On *Simchat-Torah* they would put little flags in our hands with an apple on top, the fruit of our orchards, and above it, stuck in the apple, a small, lighted candle. Because of the elements of folklore in the holiday, we could see how the Bible fitted in with the tilling of the soil and its cheering fecundity. It was only on those holidays that Papa went to the synagogue. At other times he never showed his face there. Although he was well versed in Jewish lore, he frequently found himself involved in theological arguments with the religious officials of the village, the slaughterer and the cantor, especially when the latter was an outsider who had been brought in to lead the prayers on the High Holy Days. In those arguments he would defend the ethical values and the rationalism of Mosaic and Rabbinical law, while objecting to its ritualistic and mystical aspects. He accepted what it had to say on the matter of human relations, but was skeptical about the relations between man and God.

The holidays were followed by the rains and winter. To this very day I regain the immediate awareness of a child every time I sniff the fragrance of the arid ground absorbing the first rain. Sometimes we were so exhilarated by the cultivated soil that we would flatten ourselves on the earth, take a handful of soil and chew it. The earth was clean. And the possibly unexplainable fact is that I considered it tasty.

In the manner of farmers everywhere, we lifted our eyes to the heavens and prayed to the One who causes the rain to fall.

Towards seeding time, there was the never-ending controversy between two schools of farmers: which was better? To sow the fields before the first rain or after? Before the first rain, you had the advantage of a considerable rainfall which would fill out the seeds and assure you of an early sprouting; however, if the next rain was slow in coming, the sprouts would wither and then your only alternative was a second seeding, in the middle of winter. Those in favor of sowing the fields after the first rain contended that their method was less risky, and moreover while seeding they could destroy the sprouting weeds; but there was a catch to it: the time remaining for the grain to grow was shorter. They had a hard time deciding, and I too have yet to determine which is the better course.

Between one rain and the next we would sow the winter grains, prune the vineyard, plow and cultivate between the rows, trim the almond trees; and in the end, when all tasks were done and winter was in evidence and the weeds began to grow, together with the rest of the farmers we used to send our cows, mules, horses and donkeys out to the great meadow which lay in the vicinity of the oak forest northwest of the village, the area which is now occupied by Kibbutz Bet-Keshet. The farmers used to joke about sending the animals on "vacation." We called that area *yaar* (forest) while the Arabs called it *vaar*, meaning a field of rocks or a wood of oaks. To tell the truth, it had plenty of both.

The animals spent some two months in the natural pasture without returning home, with only the Arab herdsmen for company. The herds returned at the end of the winter season, towards spring. It was a fine sight to see the hundreds of animals galloping in lively rhythm, with their mooing and bleating and neighing and braying combined as they interrupted one another, collectively creating some special, invigorating sort of music which no stranger would understand. Stamping their hoofs on village ground, the animals strode down the main street and abruptly turned aside, herd by herd under their own initiative, into the open gates of the yards, each herd in the yard of its master. One might truly say: "The ox knows its owner and the ass its master's crib." The owners themselves stood at the gate, counting their livestock and checking them all to see that none were missing and that they had returned in good shape. It was a touching scene, that meeting between old friends, the farmers and their animals back home. During the months of pasturage and leisure the animals had put on flesh, and their skin was clear and glossy. At times one cow or another would be followed by a toddling calf, small and embarrassed, which would enter the barn in its mother's wake, gaping at its new abode. With the herds back in the village it seemed as if spring itself had returned.

At this point something must be said about "Henry"—may a righteous bull's memory be blessed—who was shipped from distant England to our remote village in order to improve our local breed of cows and increase their milk yield. Henry was a bull such as we had never seen,

with his brown, gleaming hide and his horns of imposing size and shape. He was tall and stout and his cloven hoofs were wide as footballs. Between his rear legs, two gigantic, impressive testicles swayed within their pouch. In a word, he was a bull to be proud of, from the land where great bulls grow. But that was precisely the trouble: he was too big and heavy to be born on the backs of our small, skinny native cows, without them falling flat. The difference in height between the two breeds did nothing to facilitate their mating either. However, the farmers and Henry's master—who was on the agricultural staff of the mandatory government—were not to be daunted. They took counsel and arrived at a solution: a special wooden structure with an elevated floor. The little Arab cow was led into this structure from which there was no escape and there she waited, held fast in the trap, for the giant bull to rear up and fulfill her every wish, and his as well. He performed his task slowly, calmly, unlike the local bulls which were smaller and more agile and gave vent to their desire with energetic fervor, prancing on their hind legs as their forelegs struggled to get a good grip on the excited cow's body till the coveted copulation was attained. To the onlooker—and we looked at that act of procreation with wide-open eyes—it seemed as if Henry was merely doing his duty as an educated bull should, with no excess of ardor, as if he were a disciplined circus animal executing his trainer's commands.

Unlike their Arab neighbors, the Jewish farmers were anxious to improve the breeds of their livestock. So it was that a communal billy goat of the tall, muscular Damascus breed was acquired and introduced into the flock of small, black local goats, which were scrawny and poor in milk. His job was easy, but that was not the case with the splendid, heavy ram which had been imported with his thick, kinky wool from somewhere in Turkey or the Balkans.

Even a ewe in heat, pining for her partner, had a hard time moving her heavy tail aside, and the immigrant ram, unlike his local counterparts, had a hard time as well. More than once a shepherd's "intervention" was called for, he removing the obstacles with his own hands or aiming the "arrow" at its "target." Such scenes, which are the common lot of every country boy, made us sensually alert, aware from an early age of the sexual festival carried on by nature in every season of the year.

A particularly important event, which excited adults and youngsters alike, was the arrival in our village of the big stallion and the gigantic jackass which had been raised in the experimental government farm in Acco for the express purpose of breeding. They would come with their trainers and stay in our midst for two weeks or so, till the "festival" was over.

The stallion was of pure Arab stock, tall and well-formed, quick-footed and splendidly trained. His brown hide gleamed and his thick mane was trimmed to perfection, and between his ears—as a sort of decorative trademark advertising his function and powers—sprouted an artificial curl made of hardened hair. The farmers who wanted a colt or filly would conduct their lovely mares to the pampered stallion's bower of bliss. Those who wanted a mule would conduct them to the sturdy grey jackass' bower of bliss. The crossbreeding of jackasses and mares—so similar and so different—produces an offspring which, though sterile, is tall as a horse, patient as a donkey and as strong as both, qualities which are quite indispensable in the hard labor of farming.

The studhorse's neigh, the whinnies of the mare as she calmed; the braying of the jackass, whose task was all the more difficult since he was shorter than the mare—such were the ingredients of the great occasion in the life of the village, and many farmers, even those who had nothing to do there, used to come and watch the annual event. At times women came too, but they observed the scene from a distance or even in hiding. We children used to run away from school and gaze, open-mouthed and breathless, at the thrilling scene which played on the senses and inflamed the imagination. At times the adults tried to remove us from the "bower of bliss"; nevertheless, they as well, being the products of the puritanical Jewish town and the first generation of Jewish farmers on their own land, could not conceal their obvious enjoyment: they grinned, chuckled and told jokes, assuming a practical tone when discussing the "results," while the blush on their cheeks revealed what was often in their hearts—a deeply rooted uneasiness at this peeping of theirs into the forbidden realm of sex.

During most of the winter our village was cut off, rather like a desert island at times. There was little work to be done. While it poured outside we sat about the fireplace, which was made of clay, fixing our eyes on the glowing charcoal that warmed the room and our hearts as well. Sometimes on a winter's night the youngsters would get together in the village clubhouse, whether for a talk or a passionate dance to the music of the mandolin, recorder and harmonica. The days of inactivity in the fields were used for the repair of our tools; the mules' harnesses and the horses' saddles were mended and rubbed with resin; the barns, stables and sheepcote were given a thorough cleaning, in anticipation of the herd's return.

In the breaks between the rains the villagers would pop out of their houses, wearing heavy winter coats and rubber boots, and congregate in the main street to enjoy a bit of sunlight and conversation.

◈ ◈

At the end of the rainy season, spring launched its assault on the fields, mountains and mankind. The fields were given a final plowing at a feverish pace with the double-share plow, which left no clods behind it, and the summer crops were sown with precision and a prayer, as was the farmers' practice year after year, seeing that these seeds would have to grow without rain, aided only by the dew and the moisture stored in the ground. In the days between the end of winter and the beginning of spring the earth, covered with a green quilt, would be split from its depths by a host of wondrously colorful flowers.

But of all the blossoms, Nature shaped none more beautiful or intoxicating than the pink and white flower of the almond tree, to say nothing of the hundreds of dunams of almond groves which became, for a few weeks every February, enormous flower gardens.

I remember the Kefar Tavor summer as a hot season big with fruit, grain fields tall as a man, and their harvest: the tremendous stacks in the grain shed; the threshing, done with a sledge; separating the chaff from the grain with a wooden winnowing fan; appraising the grain crop and picking the olives; the smell of the tobacco as it dried; filling sacks for storage and the market; picking grapes and almonds; the various kinds of fruit which appeared in our village, in boxes rocking on the backs of donkeys driven by the local Arabs. I've already mentioned their coming to us from well-watered Bikat Bet-Netofa; from them we used to buy fruit and other crops which we couldn't afford to grow ourselves, such as pomegranates, figs and juicy watermelons. Our precipitation was poorer than theirs, and the variety of our crops was limited accordingly. We concentrated on the chief and most profitable yields, considering our conditions and manpower. The peddlers' voices mingled with the other sounds of summer in the village of my birth, and their fruit made an appetizing contribution to our moonlit nights in the grain shed, the nights of guard duty and love as we used to sing in those days, which are etched in my memory.

Most of the year, our days were devoted to work. We worked hard and if we were tired, it was with the good kind of fatigue that plunges one into deep sleep, from which he awakens limber and refreshed. Very early, at dawn, we would rise for work on the farm and in the fields, packing provisions for ourselves and the animals, including drinking water, and setting off.

We suffered greatly from the harsh climate: in the winter the east winds would slap us in the face, the powerful *Sharkiot* which split the skin and drove through our gloves as well, till our fingers were numb; in the summer it was the heat waves and the gnats, which nothing could discourage, neither the white shawls we wrapped about our heads nor the oil with which we rubbed our face and ears. The workday did not terminate with our return home towards evening. There were many tasks yet to be done, in the barn, the stable, the henhouse, the yard, after which came guard duty, by shifts, in the vineyard or the village itself.

I don't remember whose idea it was to feed the work animals an early breakfast, precisely at four in the morning. Sometimes after filling their troughs I would linger awhile in a corner of the stable and listen to them munching the barley with their big, strong teeth. I would still be half asleep, heavy-eyed, but even so it was pleasant to sit there in the corner, in the warm darkness of the stable filled with the warm breath of the champing animals, and to listen to that extraordinary nocturnal symphony playing in the air. When they finished their portion, I would take a brush and begin scrubbing and combing the animals, before they were harnessed.

The days flew by and the seasons passed in succession. Our lives revolved in a definite orbit, constantly tinged with a sense of loneliness which was a significant factor in the attitude of Kefar Tavor's inhabitants. How we rejoiced in every guest who turned up in our village! If we were informed in advance of the arrival of guests or relatives, we would set out by wagon to meet them at the train station in Afula or at a predetermined spot on the Haifa-Tiberias highway.

In this connection, a few words must be devoted to Masud, the Jew from Tiberias who was our chief link with that city. Once a week he would appear in the village, followed by a train of plodding mules laden with every good thing: the mail, household necessities, everything from medicine to garments. Owing to their isolation from the centers of population, the village women were generally obliged to rely on affable Masud's good taste when choosing the beautiful shawl or kerchief which they would order through him for an approaching holiday or family event. Masud's visit became a weekly attraction in the life of our remote village, and his appearance was a good enough reason to let one's tools lie idle awhile in the yard or to leave off studying in school. Everyone raced to the local council ḥall in anticipation of a letter or desired commodity, as well as the equally important chance to sell his own farm products to Masud, before the others beat him to it.

◈ ◈

The better part of our harvest from the fields and almond groves was marketed in Haifa or Nazareth, to dealers with whom we did a steady business, both Jews and Arabs. At the end of summer, when the threshing in the grain shed was done and a part of the wheat, barley and legumes had been set aside for the next year's seeding, and for home and livestock consumption as well—the latter including the chickens which noisily roamed the village yards, with a few ducks and geese waddling among them here and there—we would load most of the harvest on mule-drawn wagons, driven by ten or so of the village youngsters, and set off, generally in the afternoon, in a long caravan bound for Haifa. We would travel all night, reaching Haifa only at noon the next day. On the way we would stop at predetermined sites, usually close to water sources but not especially in the settlements, which in those days were few enough; there we would water the animals, eat our fill, rest a little, smoke an aromatic cigarette and set off again. That journey together, by caravan, was our means of security against bandits, of whom there was no shortage, and it gave us the advantage of mutual protection and aid in times of need. To draw a comparison, one might say that those were the wagon trains of the Israeli "Wild East." Just as we left the village, armed and united, so we returned, always together.

We utilized our stay in Haifa by stocking up on the vital necessities which we would need during the long "winter siege." At wholesale prices, we bought whatever could be stored and preserved at home without spoiling: clothing, boxes of lump sugar, blocks of halvah, little barrels of herrings; cans of smoked fish, sardines, a few dozen cans of beef from Australia; salt, kerosene and other such commodities which were absolutely essential. We preferred to buy our olive oil from our Arab neighbors, since the product of their primitive oil presses retained the olive's pungent flavor.

Our encounter with the big city set the stage for bold, impressive experiences which enriched our treasury of stories for many days to come. With the eager wonderment of country boys, we drank in the bustling streets with their people and vehicles. We would stare at length at the shop windows, which our longing eyes saw as the quintessence of beauty and elegance. Though instructed in thriftiness from childhood, we permitted ourselves to "run wild" a bit on every trip, even wasting a bit of money on little thrilling amusements like a visit to the "Jolly Park," which was what they used to call the roofless cinema showing silent films, whose screen stood among the trees and water fountains of lower Haifa. We had to stretch our imaginations a good deal in order to make sense out of the screened escapades. But then the movies, though silent and sometimes blurred, provided an occasion for a little bittersweet ice cream, which was also impossible to get in our village.

A trip to the "Jolly Park" might remind us of the Arab who used to appear in our village once every few months, with a "magic box" on his back and a tripod in his hand. On one of the streetcorners he would set up the tripod, attach the *Sanduk Agmi* (Persian Box) to it, and for half an Egyptian penny or two eggs he would let us enter the wondrous, enchanted realm of the Orient. Through a round glass we would observe the splendors of Persia, the pyramids of Egypt, feasting our eyes on the minarets of Damascus, the mighty warriors casting their lances at dreadful dragons, and naked women as well—one picture after another, the Arab's hand turning the reel of film while his mouth kept up a running, rhymed account of what we viewed.

There were other, nearer markets, chiefly Nazareth, to which we used to go in different seasons. In order not to flood the market and thus bring about an abrupt drop in prices—nobody in those days had heard anything about subsidies—we refrained as far as possible from the concentrated marketing of our produce in a single city at the same time, especially as the yield of little Kefar Tavor was great and abundant, since in spite of its small size it held an extensive area of rich soil, rather like a miniature breadbasket.

If my memory doesn't deceive me, I was five years old the first time I went to Nazareth. And the first trip only

Shirley Hirsch 1974

whetted my appetite—I would do anything not to miss another opportunity to go there. Whenever I was able to, I accompanied my father or my big brothers on their frequent trips to the district capital. The way we entered the city of churches and crosses; our introduction to the vivid, Oriental market, crowded and smelly and loud; our stay there for long hours at a time—such were the things which attracted me but also affected me with a strange sense of foreignness and sometimes even hostility. Apparently my school studies and the stories of the suffering the Jews had undergone at the hands of the Crusaders, the Inquisition's horrors, the expulsion of the Jews from Spain—all these had left their mark on me. They erected an invisible but distinct barrier between me and everything that smacked of Christianity, though this had no effect on my human relations with Christians, many of whom were regular guests in our home. I took an entirely different attitude toward Islam, regarding which I had no store of deterring grievances. To this day I remember how I refrained from bending over when facing the church, so that I wouldn't catch myself kneeling to a crucifix. This prohibition which I intentionally enforced on myself became rather demanding when I was required to stand a sack of grain or almonds on end in the wagon, in order to ease it onto the porter's shoulders. At such times I used to lower myself on my toes, bending my knees and making sure my head and back were held as straight as possible.

◈ ◈

Like all farmers, my father was a busy man. And like all children, I enjoyed traveling in my father's company. To this day I remember with a clarity undimmed by time the few trips we took together to Mount Tabor. With Papa along, the ascent to the summit was always slower, which was due not so much to any clumsiness of his as to the way he had of walking, a naturally slow pace. Holding himself erect, he would walk with a deliberate tread, waving the cane which he'd made himself, a useful object both for support and self-defense. Once he started walking, whether to Mount Tabor or his distant fields, his pace never changed—slow, measured steps which he kept up even when the hike went on for many miles. I don't know why, but somehow I always picture him wearing work clothes with a peaked cap on his head. If it was summer, his outfit would be composed of trousers whose color had more gray to it than blue, and a shirt with the sleeves rolled up; if it was winter, he would add a dark brown jacket, which he'd remove before beginning his work.

On my trips with Papa to Mount Tabor we used to stop off on the mountainside, paying a visit to the sheik of the Arav A-Zabiach Bedouin tribe. They were old acquaintances and between one fight and the next good friends as well. Papa was careful not to bypass his tent whenever we happened to be in the tribal area. If we arrived in the morning, we would stay a little while, sipping a small cup of bitter coffee as required, but if it was close to noon we couldn't take our leave without partaking of a hearty lunch first, in compliance with our gracious hosts.

I don't remember that Papa ever accompanied us on our trips to the wadis. They were generally undertaken exclusively by the younger set, whether on foot or riding our horses and donkeys. The donkeys served us children as a means of transportation when doing our chores and also for long trips far from the village. Riding them was a good way of preparing oneself for promotion, namely to the horse, a pleasure which was denied us till our tenth year. Not that we disdained the donkeys: we knew that Messiah was to come not on horseback but on a donkey, but even so we used to count the years in wistful eagerness, sighing for the taller animal with the beautiful neck and long legs.

And they were so different to ride on: while we used to sit as far back as possible on the donkey, on account of its odd, unsteady legs, we rode the horse with our heads closer to its own.

In addition to draft animals, our village had not a few noble riding horses whose neighing could be heard from the farmyards. We had a particularly noble mare, a thoroughbred which was purchased—I don't remember from whom—in Gaza. The Arabs named her Al-Azavieh, in other words the Gazian, but we called her Adina (the Delicate One), and she was just like her name. She was esteemed for her origin and characteristics as one of the best horses in the Galilee, and more than once my brothers had her to thank for the victories they achieved in the horse races, in which Jews and Arabs participated, at the weddings which were held with much ceremony in the Bedouin camps. Papa used to ride her too. However, he usually did so for a definite purpose, to have a look at some field or orchard. It was otherwise with us, his sons, since we just liked to ride her, for pleasure. Sometimes I would race her through a village street in order to show off as well, especially in front of any city girls who happened to be in our village on a class trip. On one of those gallops my luck ran out and the saddle strap suddenly came apart. Both of us, saddle and rider, made a hard landing on the ground. The signs of that fall are evident to this day on one of the fingers of my left hand. As for the rest of my body, it was perfectly battered. The well-trained mare stopped and my brother Zvi, who was passing by, rushed to my aid. We were still busy washing my wounds when who should appear but Papa. I don't remember if he gave my wounds so much as a glance, but I remember the calm tone of voice in which he said: "You don't need a saddle. It's only good for long rides. You're better off without it when you gallop."

Shirley Hirsch 1974

"All right, Papa," I replied; "I'll do it that way . . . tomorrow."

"Not tomorrow, right now," Papa decreed and added, "get on the horse, go ahead, don't be afraid, ride over to the pharmacy."

Like it or not, I mounted the horse, while my body groaned in pain. Papa loved me, this I knew, but his reactions were always restrained and Spartan. My brother Eliav has an entirely different story to tell concerning my father's reactions to another childhood accident of mine:

"When he was four or five years old . . . we were returning at noon from a trip and he ran towards our wagon, tried to climb up on it and slipped and fell and the front wheel ran over his chest. The doctor was summoned at once, and Papa stood over him with a pistol in his hand and yelled: "If you don't save this boy you're as good as dead!" Fortunately for us and the doctor it turned out that the boy wasn't injured, and peace was restored."

This engaging tale might very well bring a smile to the reader's lips, but anyone who was acquainted with Papa would surely sympathize with that poor doctor.

The raising of expensive riding horses went gradually out of fashion, but even then my father agreed, out of consideration for me, knowing my fondness for horses, to let us keep Adina's daughter, Kochava (Star), who was so named for the white star on her brown forehead. From then on I had the good fortune, at Bar-Mitzvah age more or less, to raise my own filly and train her as well, I being her only rider. She stayed with me till the time came for me to go off to the Kaduri agricultural school, when she was sold. Much to my satisfaction, on my arrival at Kaduri I was entrusted, on the strength of my experience, with the raising and training of another filly, Aviva, who was no less beautiful or lightfooted than her predecessors.

Aviva's training is a story in itself: first of all, I refused to let my schoolmates take care of her. I myself would feed her, scrub her, take her out of the stable and bring her back. One day, when the time seemed ripe to me, I asked my friend Arnan to ride her mother while I mounted Aviva for the first time. It was my hope that during the ride Aviva would conform to her mother's gait, but to my amazement, before I'd even managed to get properly settled on her, without a saddle, she broke out in a wild gallop, racing up the hillside towards the school's athletic field. I knew I wouldn't be able to stop her, and on the other hand jumping off her, in the midst of that frantic dash, was a sure way of breaking my bones. Therefore I decided to hang on and let her gallop out to the open range, till her strength failed. On the way I passed by our principal, Shlomo Tsemach, his wife and also—his daughter, Ada. Mrs. Tsemach, a physician with whom I was friendly, let out a frightened scream: "Yigal, be careful!" What with the principal's eyes on me, his wife's concern and the presence of his daughter (another reason not to fall), I felt an urge to put on a good show, without a chance of failure. The rebellious filly's dash had meanwhile taken us up to our athletic field, which was covered with muddy puddles, the remains of the last rain, dull watery mirrors at every turn. With all my might I tried to steer her over to the field. It worked. My classmates who were playing there froze in place, and with a worried but rather admiring glance they followed the rebellious filly's swift debut. The frantic climb up the hill and the damp, soft ground had taken their toll, and little by little the filly's gait slackened. I seized the opportunity and instead of stopping her I used my spurs and the bit in her mouth to keep her galloping. The spent filly gathered the last of her strength and made a final effort to quicken her gait, but her strength failed her; she stopped with her head held low, a sign of submission. After resting a few minutes I turned her around and at a slow, measured pace, in perfect obedience, she made her way back to the stable. The war of attrition was over. She accepted my authority, and from then on all I had to do was train her to gallop at a normal pace.

Chapter 5

I'VE ALREADY described our home, its interior and yard. Now is the time to say something about the appearance of the street on which it stood. The street was quite straight and enclosed by a stone wall, the latter having been formed, as I've mentioned, by connecting the outer walls of the barns, the sheepcotes and the other farm buildings which occupied the yards of the village; the wall contained gates which could be locked and bolted at night. It was with good reason that the older settlements in the Galilee and other regions of Israel surrounded themselves with protective walls. Their inhabitants were well acquainted with the human environment in which they had made their homes; moreover, the Jewish farms were fruitful and thriving and there was no lack of hostile, aggressive elements who were always ready to lay hands on Jewish life and property, whether their motives stemmed from greed or nationalism. For that reason it was essential to adopt suitable provisions for security, and in those days a wall of that sort was regarded as a proper strategic countermeasure against the gang raids, which were made on foot or horseback with the support of small arms alone. Furthermore, although the adult male population of the village spent their nights within the walls, their days were largely passed in the open fields. Hence it was no wonder that when departing for the distant fields the adults wanted to leave their families within the walls, which would be a firm, sure base for their defense and also afford the adults a refuge to which they could return when necessary. Such villages, enclosed by walls, with a barbed-wire fence a little farther out, were the fortresses of those days, but by no means could they be considered ghettos, and there was no similarity, not even a coincidental one, between those villages and the ghettos of the East European or Middle Eastern type.

Actually it was only the outer wall which served as a defense barrier, a double wall, thick and extremely strong. The stone or concrete walls which divided the yards and farm plots were built not for security reasons but rather against the "evil eye" of one's neighbors, and out of an aspiration to live one's life in the greatest possible privacy, rather than in the public view. The part of the yard which faced the main street was also blocked off with a wall, and every yard had a gate of its own, whereas the front of the house, which we called the "front garden," was merely fenced in, either with a wire partition or thorn bushes and even stones. Needless to say, the gardens were not identical in appearance. Some were lovelier than others, in keeping with the owner's taste or skill. Beyond the wall every farmer had a four-dunam plot for raising forage and hay for domestic consumption. For some reason we called this plot "the bottom garden." A wicket or narrow gate led out to it from the yard.

◆ ◆

More than once during my childhood I was an eyewitness to real physical combat in which my father employed the tactics of a wrestler—against Arabs who had trespassed on his property or a shepherd who had rashly driven a few goats onto a patch of his land. For a minute my blood would run cold, but the outcome was always a wonder: my father would flatten his opponent and force him to surrender.

I particularly remember one hard fight. My participation consisted of no more than an unsuccessful attempt to throw a stone at the two Arabs who were grappling with my father. That morning we had taken the wagon and gone off to a field about three kilometers north of the village, in order to gather the wheat that had been cut the day before. We usually did the reaping in the afternoon, when the grain was dry, and picked it up in the early dawn, when it was damp with dew and the kernels wouldn't split and there was little danger of losing any on the way.

As we approached the field we saw two Arabs sitting by the road while their horses, which were tied to stones, munched the ears of our cut barley. The material damage was slight; after all, how much could the two horses have eaten at such an early hour? But my father boiled with indignation at the audacious encroachment on his land. And by whom? Two strangers who were just passing by; not an Arab friend who would have been tolerated somehow if he had presumed to do such a thing. My father raised his voice and demanded that they get their horses out of the field at once. If they had stood up and taken their horses and gone, the incident would have ended without a quarrel. But one of them had a loose tongue and he greeted my father with a round of Arab curses. My father jumped off the wagon while it was still moving—the exchange had taken place before we reached the field. He grabbed a pitchfork and charged them. I stopped the mules and ran after him, in case he needed help—I was seven or eight years old at the time—and when I arrived he was already wrestling with one of them, while the other tried to get a hold on him from behind. The time had come for me to intervene in what might be described as my first engagement in battle: I gathered up some pebbles and began throwing them at the other Arab. I was careful not to hit my father, but I didn't hit the Arab either. I picked up the pitchfork which my father had thrown as he ran, but there was no need for it. Although my father never took a training course in the Palmach and had no instruction in the art of judo, it took him two minutes to pin down the first Arab, with whom he was wrestling; then, with an unexpected, unorthodox move, while still bent over his outstretched, screaming opponent, he grabbed the other Arab's legs in one hand and laid him flat as well. It goes without saying that my father had a pistol in his pocket, but he didn't draw it. What the Arabs had in their pockets I never discovered. They got up, took their horses and beat a shameful retreat. The next minute some local Arabs arrived, neighbors who were well acquainted with my father and had also been eyewitnesses to his fight, and they congratulated him on his victory.

"Why didn't you draw the pistol?" I asked him and he replied: "A shot might have resulted in the Arab's death, and the killing of an Arab starts off a blood feud that could go on for many years. Since we have to live here, we should use our hands or a pitchfork, so long as it's possible. The pistol is for when you have no choice, when your life is in danger." I remember that not only as an example of personal courage—and my father was renowned for his courage throughout the Galilee—but also as my first lecture on the considerations involved in the use of arms. Even when tempers raged my father knew how to control himself and behave as the situation demanded, doing no more than was necessary. Since he was so brave, I often asked him if he was never afraid. "The man who's never afraid is a fool," he would reply. "The trick is to know how to control your fear. You're not the only one who's afraid; Muhammed is too. The question is who's going to be the first to get the better of his fear, you or Muhammed."

It wasn't by speeches that my father educated us, but by his personal example and tests. Two of those tests, one of them involving my brothers Zvi and Eliav, and the other myself, are worth telling about.

Eliav relates:

"It was a Sabbath day during an oppressive heat wave, the harvest season for the almonds we had planted in our plot close to the village. In the early afternoon my brother Zvi asked me to take a look at the almond grove, to make sure there were no thieves there. I was a boy of ten. As I reached the grove I saw four or five young Bedouin picking sackfuls of almonds from the trees. I went straight back home and asked my twelve-year-old brother to help me, hoping that together we might be able to overpower at least one of them. Papa was having his afternoon nap and we didn't want to wake him. So we ran out, both of us, to the almond grove, and from a distance we saw that two big sacks were already full to the top. The Arabs noticed us and picked up their heels and made off for their tribal tents, leaving their booty behind them in the grove. 'Al-Ansari's sons are after us!' they yelled as they fled, and we pursued them. Four of them scattered every which way but Zvi kept after the fifth boy and chased him right up to one of the sheik's tents.

" '*Ana tanibak, Hasheik*,' ('You are my refuge, Sheik,' ") yelled the young Arab who sought asylum within the tent; however, my brother Zvi ignored the sacred code which stipulated that whoever sought asylum in a Bedouin tent was immune to injury, and all the more so in the tent of a sheik—he burst into the tent, with little me in tow, and dragged the boy outside to take his punishment. The sheik, who considered himself offended, tore out one of the pegs that supported the tent and lifted it to land a blow on Zvi's head, since my brother had broken the sacred law of tradition on pain of death.

" '*Armi al aseh!*' ('Let go of the stick!') A mighty bellow was heard all at once from my father, who appeared as if he'd dropped out of the sky. With my own eyes I saw the bristling sheik let his hand fall, so afraid was he of the Ansari.

"Then we all went in to the sheik's tent and sat with our legs folded on the rugs, mattresses and pillows which had been customarily spread in our honor, and in my father's presence the sheik gave vent to his displeasure at what my brother had done in forcibly removing a seeker of asylum from his tent. To this my father replied that his son had committed a grave offense indeed, but it should be remembered that he too was a victim of injustice, since those boys had tried to steal almonds from his trees and even raised a hand to one of his sons, an act which could not be easily forgiven. In the end Papa agreed to bury the hatchet and accept the sheik's promise that if such a thing were to happen again the sheik would punish the offender with his own hands, with one of our family as witness. Thus we parted in friendship—till the next spat.

"It was only when we were home again that Papa told us how he'd noticed my brother and me dash out of the house and had hurried after us, trying to keep out of our sight. That way he could be close by to protect us from injury and also to see for himself how his sons reacted, and if they really were unflinching in the face of danger. We scored a success: he was pleased with us." *

And as for my test:

When I attained the bar-mitzvah age of thirteen, my father summoned me to the grain shed at the rear of the

* Eliav Peikovitz (Allon): *Masechet Shel Bazelet*.

yard and said: "By putting on phylacteries you haven't yet fulfilled all the principal commandments; you've become a man, and from now on you're going to have your own weapon." As he spoke he pried open a metal can and took out a semiautomatic Browning pistol, wrapped in a woolen napkin. "It was mine; from now on it's yours. You're going to clean it and take care of it. You already know how to use it. There's no license for it and its place is here in the shed, behind the wheat bin." I was very excited. This was the day I'd dreamed about, longing for the time I'd have my own personal weapon like my brothers, and needless to say my father. I was still in the grip of my excitement when he added: "Tonight you're going out to guard what's left of the sorghum harvest in *Balut*, since we haven't had time to bring it in to the barn yet."

That distant field, at the northern end of the village lands, had, as did all our other fields, an Arab name: *Balut*, meaning oak tree. In the middle of its two sections, in a rocky spot, grew our sturdy, beautiful oaks.

As I said, I was perfectly thrilled, but I put on a knowing, courageous air and just after sunset took out my very own pistol, hid it in my shirt and set out to the north, in the direction of the *Balut* field which was close to the present site of Kibbutz Bet-Keshet. The field bordered on a dirt road, more like a path, which went from Tzemach in the Jordan Valley to Nazareth. It was actually the main road from the Houran across the Jordan to the sea. For the first time in my life I was the sole guard of a field, alone beneath the starry sky through which a full moon of autumn drifted. The farther I got from the village, the greater was my fear. I had about four and a half kilometers to walk, and by eight o'clock, maybe a little later (in those days I didn't own a watch yet), I reached the field, which I knew quite well. At once I installed myself beneath an oak tree, behind a large rock. That was my first tactical

error, actually two errors: a rock doesn't provide good cover from rifle bullets, because of the ricochets; and a big tree, with the many birds that pass the night among its branches, doesn't make a good hiding place. From time to time the birds were startled, and then they would noisily shake the branches and leaves. I trembled at the noise and managed to tolerate it only with the greatest of difficulty. I considered moving to another place, but once I'd gripped the earth, which afforded me a measure of security, I remained where I was. Little by little the tension lessened and I began to get used to the darkness and solitude. My ears opened to receive the stirrings of the night: the gusts of wind among the leaves and bushes, the shrill chirp of the crickets and the sound of the frogs croaking at a little distance, by a muddy spring. If I had a prayer in my heart it was only that the thieves should refrain that night from trying to filch the remains of our harvest.

After midnight I heard caravans passing on the path next to the field. The travelers didn't notice me and I let them pass. Thank God they didn't try to fill their sacks with our crops. But later, it might have been two o'clock, I made out three men on horseback straying from the path and invading the field. Less than fifty meters away from me they dismounted and began filling their sacks with sorghum. Their attitude suggested utter confidence: they spoke aloud and one of them even cracked a joke, his two friends laughing. The test was on.

Before my departure my father had told me that if thieves should approach, I was first to let them get on with their work and only later to sound a warning in Arabic; if my cry didn't faze them, I was to fire a shot in the air. "But remember," he warned me, "be careful not to hit them. Don't be a hothead. Take aim only if they try to get close to you."

I followed his instructions to the letter. I overcame my fear. Papa's orders helped but so did logic: they were standing while I lay behind a rock, and even though it was, I repeat, not the best sort of cover, my situation was better than theirs; they didn't know I existed and I had the advantage of surprise. So I did two things at once: I raised my voice, rather a childish voice to which I tried to give a mature ring as far as possible—after all I was thirteen!—and I yelled "*Andak!*" and at the same time I cocked my pistol with a metallic click, so as to frighten them. I hoped the horsemen would let go of the sacks, jump on their horses and flee for their lives. To my amazement, which was mixed with dread, they took up positions in the field and one of them responded with a battle cry. For the first time in actual combat I pulled the trigger. The pistol fired properly, into the air of course. The response was a rattle of weapons but no shots. What now, I asked myself, what next? Should I aim at them? And what if one of them is killed? What if I'm killed? Maybe it would be better to withdraw under the cover of darkness? In other words to flee? Such were the thoughts that rapidly shot through me; but in the same split second I heard all at once, somewhere behind me, a little to the flank, cries and hearty curses in Arabic, with a distinct Russian accent. Immediately after them came rifle shots in the air, above the heads of the horsemen who jumped on their horses and disappeared into the night, leaving their half-full sacks behind. I gave a sigh of relief. Needless to say, the figure darting out at me was Papa's.

Yes, he wanted to test my courage, but he loved me enough—sometimes even too much—to let me go it alone. Just as he'd followed Zvi and Eliav, he'd gone after me without my noticing, taken a position in a suitable spot and let me fend for myself. Only when he was sure I was in real danger did he intervene, and it was his critical intervention, of course, which turned the tide. That night I learned that reserve forces are a decidedly positive factor, even when the battle is between individuals.

"We scored a success," wrote Eliav in describing the test he and Zvi had passed; "he was pleased with us." The same could be said for me. My joy that night was twofold: not only had I passed the test, but Papa *saw* me pass it. It's hard to imagine how I could have looked him in the face if I hadn't acted as I did.

Some sixteen years after that event I stood on a lawn at Israel Defense Forces Headquarters in Ramat-Gan, for the swearing-in of the first generals in our army. The then

Prime Minister and Minister of Defense, David Ben-Gurion, had decreed with his characteristic resolve that we change our foreign names to Hebrew ones, before they were made public. I accepted his demand, but how could I find a name that would please my father and the entire clan, since even in name alone I had no wish to cut myself off from them, and on the other hand there was no time to ask their advice? True, as a boy I'd wanted to adopt a new name, Reuveni, after my father, but nothing had come of it. What name should I choose now?

Ben-Gurion declared: "Hagileadi" (my nom de guerre in the underground had been Jephthah, the biblical judge Jephthah Hagileadi). Yisrael Galili suggested "Yogev" (farmer); Yitzhak Sadeh (which means field) asked: "How about Nir?" (which means cultivated field). I listened to their suggestions but happened to recall that big oak tree (oak is *allon* in Hebrew) in the sorghum field, the tree beneath which I had my first taste of battle. I promised Ben-Gurion an answer by the time our names were to be released to the newscasters. He looked at me and pronounced: "Hagileadi!" and added at once: "You're going to conquer the Gilead." "And if I conquer Nablus will you name me Nablusi?" * I asked and he burst out laughing. "I'll decide before the newscast," I repeated. In the meantime I talked it over with my wife Ruth, who was expecting me in Tel-Aviv, and together we decided: Allon. A note which reached the newscaster a minute before his announcement settled the matter. Hearing my new name for the first time on the air, my older brothers immediately guessed what had determined their kid brother's choice. As for Papa, though he refused to change his name he was pleased with mine, since it was a part of his own land.

* An Arabic slang term for homosexual.

Chapter 6

EVERYTHING I KNOW about my father's life before he came to Israel and about his initial years here, I learned from him. Whenever he mentioned my grandfather's name, he would add: "He was really strict, even more than I." If that was what the apple had to say for itself, it was easy to guess what kind of tree it had grown on.

He was a God-fearing man, my grandfather, Yehoshua-Zvi Paicovitch, an adherent of the Anti-Hassidic movement who kept his distance from them and their rabbis, and the owner of a little store for building materials in the Lithuanian city of Grodno. That city changed rulers like a woman her dresses: the Russian rule was replaced by the Polish, and the Polish by the Lithuanian, and the Lithuanian by the Russian once again. As a devout Jew and an ardent Lover of Zion, he was not enchanted by the idea that his sons would have to serve in the czarist army and swear their allegiance to Russia, the land of the pogroms. In 1880 he packed his bags and set out with his son-in-law for Israel, where he bought a plot of land in Wadi Chanin, now Nes-Tziona, and then went back home to prepare his family for immigration. In those days the latter was usually accomplished by stages; in other words, a part of the family would be dispatched first, to set up a bridgehead and lay the foundations for the settlement of the rest.

And that is exactly what my grandfather did. Except that when he returned to Israel the next time (in 1888), he took two of his sons along. Shmuel, the eldest, who subsequently participated in the founding of Yavniel, struggled to make ends meet and when his endurance was at an end set off again for America (or "Americhka," as my father called it), in order to scrape up some money for the development of his farm. Things being what they were, he remained in America, and his descendants live there to this day. The other son whom my grandfather took with him was my father, Reuven-Yosef, who was fifteen years old.

There was quite a lot involved in the matter of that plot in Wadi Chanin, and here I'll only say this: on their arrival in Israel my grandfather discovered that the plot was no longer his. Hence the three of them went off to roam the land, working in the vineyards of Mikveh Yisrael, and as day laborers in Petach-Tikvah, Rishon-Letzion and Nes-Tziona, without a chance of rest or a place of their own. They did eventually have an inheritance but only in the Galilee, where my father turned up years later. First in Rosh-Pina, as I've mentioned, where he was a construction worker. In the Galilee he was also arrested, charged with being an illegal immigrant and jailed in Saraiyeh, the famed fortress at Safed which became the command post of Adiv Shishakli, and in whose capture I was destined to participate in 1948.

Grandfather went back to Grodno to prepare the rest of his family for immigration. A few months after reaching his city, he passed away. Grandmother, who lived on to an old age, wasn't fortunate enough to set foot in Israel either. Their sons were, but only during the period of the British Mandate. Shmuel went to America, as I've said. Papa remained alone, with his mind made up to get a foothold on the land. In time his younger brother arrived in

Israel as well, he being my beloved uncle, Hillel, who settled in Kefar-Gideon in the Jezreel Valley.

Papa passed the days of his youth in Rosh-Pina. His first impressions of the Galilee were etched in his memory and he would frequently tell me of how he had marveled at Mount Canaan, the tall, beautiful mountain which he saw as a symbol of ancient Israel's power and independence. He would often describe his solitary hikes from Rosh-Pina to the Safed area, to which he made his way through the ravines and on the slopes of the mountain, without actually entering the city. He hated cities; his ideology was thoroughly anti-urban, and village life was all he aspired to. "Fast dealers" was what he called the city dwellers, with a look of disdain on his face. He was imbued from childhood with the love of Nature, animals and growing things. It was on this plane that the relations between him and his father reached a crisis while he was still a child, in his home town on the Neman River. One time—he told me—his father found him "sinfully" playing with a little puppy, in the back yard of their home. Then and there his father rewarded him with a sound slapping on the cheek, to which he added a few words of reproach in regard to the duties of the Jewish child. And to tell the truth why should a Jewish child have anything to do with a puppy, which wasn't even considered a kosher animal, to say nothing of the waste of time which should be spent on the Study of the Law? As a protest against his punishment my father stopped praying and to the very last he was a freethinker, though he did keep up the rules of tradition, particularly out of respect for my mother, who was a God-fearing woman. I can't positively say that his attitude toward religion was simply the result of that protest against his father, who without understanding him had tried to keep him from enjoying such natural things as bathing in the river, playing with a puppy or taking care of a dovecote, things which had attracted him since early childhood. Dr. Yaakov Harozen has written about Papa's years in the country:

"The father of the Israeli Allons had his start in Judah. He worked as a laborer in Rechovot and excelled in everything he did. Before long he was renowned throughout the Jewish community of the time. After that, Reuven Paicovitch turned up in Rishon-Letzion, where he was an overseer on the Baron Rothschild's projects. Yehoshua Ausovtski, the Baron's representative, noticed the diligent youngster right away and put him in charge of important operations. . . .

"One day personnel changes were made in the settlement organization, and on being sent to Rosh-Pina the representative invited Paicovitch to join him and lend a hand with the newcomers from Romania. At that juncture the Judean laborer became a Galilean, working for the revival of the land in the region of Naphtali. And on the other side of Mount Canaan the Jews of Safed still kept to their narrow alleys. They lived a shadowy existence, many of them dependent on charity for their daily bread and subject to the rule of community and synagogue officials. In time young Paicovitch was introduced to the struggles of Elazar Rokeach against the Safed leadership. Rokeach's pamphlet and his daring, revolutionary proclamations were a guiding star for Reuven Paicovitch, who was entirely devoted to the settlement movement for which he fought boldly and whose flag he bore proudly all his life.

"As a young man in Rosh-Pina he plowed and seeded, clearing the fields of stones and breaking ground for the vineyards so as to make the Hebrew village productive and turn the Jews into farmers, living off the work of their hands. At sundown the laborer would begin 'overseeing' the roofs and marking the walls on which the beams should be laid, in order to make a solid home. In the dark of night, when Abdul-Chamid's policemen were asleep, he secretly nailed the ceilings down and presented the authorities with a finished house, whose destruction was forbidden by law (even if it had been built on the sly, without authorization from the *Kimakam* (the district governor). Thus everyone knew that Reuven the laborer could be found in the fields by day and at night, on high, in other words on the roofs. . . . No wonder the laborer's fame increased. All Rosh-Pina sought his favor. In the end he won the daughter of Rabbi Alter Shwartz (one of the first settlers in Jeona, or Gai-Oni, as they called it)—Chayah, whom he took to be his wife." *

◈ ◈

My mother was a native-born Israeli, born in Safed, the daughter of Rabbi Alter Shwartz, who was one of the founders of Rosh-Pina. It's a well-known fact that Rosh-Pina was founded not only by immigrants from Romania but also by several old residents of the city of Safed. The experts on this subject are of the opinion that my mother's family settled in Safed as long ago as the Middle Ages; however, during the previous century my grandfather's grandfather was summoned to serve a term as a rabbi in Buczacz, the home town of the novelist, Shmuel Agnon. On account of the rabbinical mission, that branch of my family quit the country, but only for a single generation, since my grandfather and grandmother, my mother's parents, who were born in Buczacz, were soon sent back by their parents to Safed, where my mother was born, thus restoring the continuity of our family's residence in

* Dr. Yaakov Harozen: *Chazon Habitnachalut Bagalil*, pp. 358–63.

Israel. My brother Eliav draws a good picture of the way the two family branches, my father's and mother's, were joined:

"One day Reuven was riding his donkey along a path on Mount Canaan, on the way to the district capital, Safed, where he had some matters to look after. What should he see but a train of donkeys (there being no other transportation at the time) coming his way from Safed to Rosh-Pina. One of the riders was a girl with black hair, very lovely to look at, and the minute he saw her he was pierced to the quick, as if an arrow had found his heart. He immediately said to himself: That's the one! I want to make a home in Israel with a woman like that! And without taking stock of things he turned his donkey around and followed the train back to Rosh-Pina. Once there, he began inquiring about the pretty girl who had captivated him, and he learned that her name was Chayah-Etil, the daughter of Rabbi Shalom Dov or as he was known in public, Rabbi Alter Shwartz; her mother's name was Leah. Her parents had arrived in Israel a long time before the Romanians who founded Rosh-Pina; they had settled in Safed, where in the year of 5636, or 1876 A.D., their daughter Chayah was born, the first child in the family. Her mother Leah was the granddaughter of the Buczacz Rabbi, a fact of which Chayah, my mother, was very proud. It wasn't long before Reuven asked for her hand and they were married in 1894."

Concerning Papa in Machanaim, Dr. Yaakov Harozen has this to say:

"Once Machanaim came into being, Reuven Paicovitch was given the task of supervising the Galicians and assisting them at home and in the fields. He fulfilled his duties faithfully, with great patience. In a calm, relaxed manner the supervisor explained to his charges what they had to do so that 'the land would yield its increase.' He instructed them in the deep ways of the roots, in order that they sucessfully raise trees and saplings. From time to time he volunteered his encouragement to the settlers, who were hard put to overcome the crises which beset Machanaim.

"But the most important thing of all, in the eyes of Supervisor Paicovitch, was the study of self-defense. Each of us was required to guard his own harvest, the fruit of his garden and his animals. He was even obliged to risk his life for their sake. And the supervisor was as good as his word. From time to time he would make the rounds of the village, mounted or on foot, night and day; then he would keep his eyes peeled to make sure no Arab shepherd let his flock overrun a grain patch "by mistake." If one of the latter happened to be caught in the fields of Machanaim, he might better have made out his last will and testament. Reuven knew how to teach the Bedouins a lesson. They used to appear in that region with their flocks, damaging the crops of Machanaim and Rosh-Pina. . . . The supervisor didn't betray the hopes of his admirers. He stood by the Galicians at home and in the field. He fought daringly for their sake and repelled all foes from Machanaim's borders, every time they tried to plunder the fields or grain sheds. That was more than thirty years before the inception of the *Hagana*. Even the *Hashomer* patrol had yet to appear in the settlements.

"Such was the situation in Machanaim. And the supervisor fortified his position in the village, which he regarded as a bridgehead for Jewish settlement. Nachalat Reuven (as Reuven Paicovitch's farm was called) was perfectly kept up, a wonder to see. . . . Paicovitch also used to visit the Arab villages. There, with the sheiks and village chiefs, he would discuss the brotherhood and friendship which ought to prevail among Jews and Arabs. We're all descendants of our father Abraham, may he rest in peace—such was the message of the bearer of peace. Heaven forbid that we desecrate our holy brotherhood. Each of us must take pains to uphold it, so that it be a shining example to Arab and Jewish farmers. On such occasions he would speak at length on the subject, explaining to all the *avadim* (dignitaries) that both nations, the Jews and the Arabs, had to live together in peace beneath the heavens of Allah may his name be praised. . . . Only with the combined forces of the two brotherly nations could we succeed in driving away the Bedouins, who darted out of the desert to damage the crops, yours and ours both. Such was the message which Paicovitch never tired of repeating. At the same time he knew how to admonish the young troublemakers who shrank from Allah's code and desecrated his name (whenever they encroached on strangers' property). They would receive their just reward if they didn't behave properly, he would say with a final warning. The supervisor of Machanaim was also familiar with all the paths and passages of the Galilee. And upon discovering that someone had broken into a barn or stable, he knew at once where to place the guilt and who would have to pay. In time they all came to see that Machanaim was indeed a stronghold held by Abu Musa (the Arabs address a man by his first son's name), and they kept their distance."

A CRUEL TURN

Once the village was vacated by the other farmers, Reuven Paicovitch remained alone. Early in the morning he would go out to the fields and at sundown he would return home scowling. The joy of life was his no more. Abandoned and isolated, he resolved to stay on and keep the place alive no matter what.

People tried to make the obstinate man understand that a single individual wasn't capable of saving Machanaim, but he would reply: At least I can do the plowing without Galicians. And if there's a little Zionist spirit left among the Lovers of Zion I won't remain alone forever. Till then I'm not going to budge.

One day Rabbi Alter appeared in the deserted village, he who was renowned throughout the Galilee as the paragon of pioneers; he faced his obstinate son-in-law and said: "Listen to me, Reuven. I know you're an intelligent man, so let me tell you: you can't carry on alone in battle! You must know that I was also among the first settlers in Gai-Oni. Like you I rushed out to the forsaken soil to cultivate and seed it. But when our strength was gone (since we were few in number) we left the place, and then returned with renewed vigor once the Romanian immigrants came to our aid.

"Together with them we resumed our mission, and it was only then that we managed to build the celebrated town of Rosh-Pina. This is a fact that you will not recognize, and you're even trying to disprove it, Therefore I must tell you: Machanaim needs many more like you! Alone, you won't be able to fill the vacuum left by the deserters. Hence you must see things for what they are and accept the commands of fate."

So said Rabbi Alter, but he received no reply. Then he decided to take another approach. He addressed his silent listener and exclaimed: "Let us presume for a minute that you're right. And I'm the one who's out of his mind. You'll go on keeping up Machanaim with your own two hands, but what right do you have to mistreat your wife and bring her to an early grave? She's in the flower of life now, but her strength is already at an end and her face is creased with age because of the suffering you have inflicted on her. . . . Where is she to find the strength to be a mother to your children? They whom you regard as your only hope and joy?"

At once the afflicted man's face changed. He grew pale as death. But his tongue was tied. A minute passed, and his eyes welled tears. Alarmed, Rabbi Alter regretted the cutting words that had escaped his lips and apparently found their mark. In his remorse he tried to change his tune and persuade his son-in-law with soft words of condolence, but the latter exclaimed: "Papa, you've accused me of cruelty toward my wife, your daughter, and I'm speechless to reply. So listen well! I'm no longer capable of going on in Machanaim. I'm going to leave, so as to put an end to my wife's suffering. I'll quit my farm and return to Rosh-Pina, but I want you to know: I shall be branded forever as the one who deserted Machanaim! This will always remain my greatest defeat."

And as Eliav tells it:

"In time, candidates were sought for the founding of the Jewish settlement at Machanaim, in the vicinity of Rosh-Pina. My parents jumped at the chance. The place was deserted, strewn with fearsome rocks, with snakes swarming everywhere. . . . Papa used to kill them by the score but to no avail; new ones constantly arrived to replace them. In spite of everything, my parents tried to hang on. The farm yields were scanty and there were very few settlers. In a short time most of them gave up and left the place. My parents stayed on alone for two years more, till they too were forced to quit the deserted village, with tears in their eyes.

"From Machanaim the family returned to Rosh-Pina, where they were given a room or two at the home of Grandfather Alter, whom they all loved. To this day I remember his long white beard, the black prayer cap he used to wear, he being an orthodox Jew, and his melodious

voice when he led the prayers in the Rosh-Pina synagogue.

"However, my father regarded the tilling of the soil as his chief aspiration and the goal of his life, and he had no wish to submit to fate. It wasn't for a man like him to relinquish his dreams!

". . . Years passed and Papa, yearning for a farm, would agree to take up no other work but farming. In the end he understood that there was no way out of accepting the additional prerequisite for farm-ownership, namely the financing of chattels. He had been promised a plot of land in one of the Baron's settlements so long as he could pay the required sum, about three hundred napoleons, which was quite a lot of money at the time. . . . How could he get hold of such a sum? After much consideration and hesitancy, Papa decided, in 1905, to go to the United States of America for a few years, in order to make some money and come back and take the promised land. He went in the spring, leaving my mother in the last months of pregnancy, as well as their three children, Moshe, Mordechai and Zvi, in grandfather's home. . . .

"Concerning his trip to America, Papa told us later that when he reached New York, after a month-long crossing from Marseilles, the many immigrants on board were met at the dock by Jewish functionaries who took them to a soup kitchen, giving them their first meal in the land of Uncle Sam and a few dollars as well, to sustain them during their first days in the strange country. But my father, who was a very proud man, was not about to accept any help or be a burden to anyone. Therefore he stood apart and waited until all the others had passed by; then he went out alone to the bustling streets of the city to find a modest hotel where he could rest from the tedious voyage.

" 'Aren't you coming with us?' asked the functionaries in Yiddish. 'After all, you're a foreigner in this country;

how can you get along without us?' 'I don't need anything,' he proudly replied; 'I have some money,' and he took out the ten napoleons he'd brought from Israel. . . . The next day the Yiddish newspapers carried the following headline: 'Independent Capitalist Arrives on Immigrants' Ship!'

"For three years he worked hard till he put together the required sum and returned to his country and family. . . . To his dying day he detested America and was reluctant to talk about the three years he'd spent there. We barely managed to squeeze a few words out of him every once in a while about what he'd undergone. . . ."

Whenever I tried to make him satisfy my curiosity about his impressions of America, which was already known as the land where the streets were paved with gold, he would shrug and sum it up in a single sentence: "Another Diaspora, it's no solution for the Jews."

As for the little bit of money he earned in America, Papa used to call it *kishkeh-gelt*. In other words, he lived there in the most straitened circumstances. Returning from the United States to Rosh-Pina, he discovered that his family had grown richer by one, Eliav—"In my absence," he said, "God was a father to him" (*Eliav* means "My God is a father" in Hebrew)—who was born a few months after his departure. Now with the money in hand he finally won the right to his own land, in Kefar Tavor, which had just been founded. On a summer's day in 1907 the belongings and equipment were packed, loaded on two mules—his first purchase—and on other, rented animals, and the family set out from my grandfather's house, bound for its own rocky farm.

Two boxes were fastened to one of the donkeys: little Eliav lay in one of them and in the other a stone was placed, as a stabilizer.

As for me, many of the most wonderful days of my

childhood were passed at my grandfather's home in Rosh-Pina, which bore a considerable resemblance to our own place in Kefar Tavor, though grandfather had a big house with two stories and a lot of space inside, it having once been a hotel. After his decease I used to spend my summer vacations at my uncle's house, my uncle Meir, my mother's brother, to whom I was particularly close.

Rosh-Pina preceded Kefar Tavor by many years and its experience was of good service to the farmers of our village in matters of construction and defense.

Chapter 7

"I DIDN'T found Mascha," Papa subsequently revealed, "but I did found Bet-Keshet. . . . How did it happen? In 1907 I went to settle in Mascha as a farmer, since I wasn't a Lover of Zion but a lover of the land from childhood; however, all I received there was a house to live in; my land was to the north, in the territory of the Zabiach Bedouins, who made their living by robbery and plunder. Those plots, which were named Um-Agabl, were seven kilometers away from home, and there was no way to reach them. No Jewish farmer had ever been there, and when the time came to go out to work after the rains the Arabs wouldn't allow anyone to cross their fields.

"That was the beginning of my conflict with the Zabiachs. I said it was my conflict, because at first we were three farmers on the same property: one was a Yemenite, the second a convert, and I was the third. We began playing cat-and-mouse with the Zabiachs: when we started out early they were informed and got up early as well, to block the way, and they were many to our few; if we started even earlier, they did too. Days and nights passed with us playing hide-and-seek, till I decided to put my foot down, since if I didn't who would. So I took out the gun I had with me and fired two shots over the Zabiachs' heads, and I warned them that the third shot would go straight for their head. They argued and shouted but in the end they gave in—and we passed through. That's the way we broke the path thirty years before it became a highway, and I'm rightfully proud of being the inaugurator of that highway, which now connects Afula and Kefar Tavor with the Kaduri school and Bet-Keshet, which were nonexistent at the time.

"After that I was well-known in those parts and regarded as a hero. Later on, when the time came for my little children to go out to their father in the fields and the young Arab troublemakers wanted to throw stones at them, as they used to do, the adults would scold them with a warning: Those children belong to Chief Rim (Reuven), and he'll get even with you." *

The truth was that his attachment to the land, his diligence and the tales of his bravery made a profound impression on the local population, Arabs, Druze and Mugrabs, and his name passed into legend among the Bedouins of the Zabiach tribe. The villagers of the Galilee respected and greatly admired him. He was at home in their tents and dwellings and they used to come to him reverently, at times in order that he sit in judgment over their internal disputes and, at others, for a cup of coffee and a bit of conversation. After his arrival in Kefar Tavor there was a change in the attitude of the local Arabs toward the little bunch of farmers whose luck it was to till the land north of the settlement. This change did not take place overnight, and it involved a succession of fights and conflicts, as the following story makes clear:

"Nachman Karniel was plowing and a Bedouin was pestering him, and Nachman was careful not to let the Bedouin get close to the side where he'd hung his gun. The Bedouin, angry at the cautious Jew who didn't trust him,

* *Fifty Years of Settlement in the Lower Galilee*, pp. 199–200.

displayed his displeasure by raising his club. But that was his misfortune—the club didn't descend, because Reuven Paicovitch appeared behind him, grabbed the club and held it fast, and not only that—he landed it just once on the Bedouin's shoulder, and the latter went down. . . . How did Paicovitch get there? He'd noticed the troublesome Bedouin from a distance and had gone after him, swift as an arrow. He had experience with such 'guests,' and from then on Paicovitch and Karniel plowed the land of Um-Agabl together and came to no harm." *

At first the Arabs refused to believe that he was a Jew, which was not surprising, since to their way of thinking the Jew had traditionally been a *wlad-al-mit*, in other words a goner, and here this person appeared in their midst who was different from what they had considered a "typical Jew." "This man isn't a Jew," they said; "it's just not possible that there are Jews like him." On the other hand, he wasn't a Moslem either, and surely not a Christian. So what was he? They racked their brains till they finally decided: Ansari! That was the new name which the local Arabs gave to Reuven Yosef Paicovitch, the son of Yehoshua-Zvi from Grodno. And why Ansari? Because in northern Syria, somewhere near the Turkish border, there was a warlike tribe which had no religion, or whose religion was unknown, either infidels or pagans, who were called Ansariyeh. And so it was that to the very last his name among them was Rim (or Ram—the Arabic for Reuven) Ansari, a fearless individual who captured their imagination and won their hearts. Even today, if you happen to be in the territory of the Zabiach tribe—after the War of Liberation only their remnants still reside in Israel—and you ask them about Rim Ansari, they'll be able to tell you exactly who he was and what he did. Naturally, they also

* *Fifty Years of Settlement in the Lower Galilee*, page 445.

named him after his sons, in keeping with Arab tradition, generally after the oldest of his sons who remained on the farm; this name was periodically changed, much to my father's sorrow, since one by one the sons moved away in their search for a new place and other sources of income. First he was called Abu Musa, then Abu Mrad; after that it was Abu Razal, and when Zvi left the village my father was called Abu Diab. Finally, when of all my brothers I alone remained on the farm, they began calling him Abu Eegel—they had trouble pronouncing the name Yigal. (Incidentally, except for my father nobody called me Yigal. The nickname by which everyone addressed me was "Yega.") When I used to pass them on the way to our fields, which were near their tents, I would hear the Arab men and women, plowmen and shepherds, saying to one another: "*Hada wlad Al-Ansari,*" meaning "That's Ansari's son." It was a name to be reckoned with throughout the Galilee, and my father's merits served me well for many years in my contacts with the Arabs. An example of this may be found in the following story by Yerucham Cohen, the intelligence officer at my staff during the campaign for the liberation of the Upper Galilee in 1948:

". . . During the period preceding Operation Broom, we were informed by our men that the small Bedouin tribe of Arav-Al-Haav, which was led by Sheik Abu-Yusef and came from the village of Tova on the Syrian border, a tribe of cattle herders and smugglers renowned for their courage, wanted to join our forces, openly. That came as a surprise to us, since our situation at the time couldn't have been worse. The news aroused Yigal's curiosity, and he decided to make a personal investigation of the sheik's motives for such a step. Yigal regarded the enlistment of the tribe as a matter of political importance which was equal in value to its military importance. An order was issued to the officer in charge of Operation

Broom, which was in full swing at the time, not to molest anyone from that tribe. To be doubly sure this was carried out, the unit which was active in that area was accompanied by a native of those parts. The visit with Sheik Abu-Yusef wasn't undertaken right away but only later.

"At the appointed time, two jeeps armed with machine guns set out for the village of Tova. Seeing that he was not yet thirty and looked even younger than his age, Yigal was afraid that when he appeared out of uniform, without any signs of rank, not to mention a mustache or boots, the sheik wouldn't believe that he was the commander of the Jewish forces. Therefore he decided to present himself as the deputy commander, who had been sent by his superior to make the acquaintance of the sheik and his men and settle the details of the agreement. Manu Friedman and I planned the visit in advance so that it would have the aspect of a ceremony, without any surprises from the Syrian side of the border.

"We arrived at the camp on time. Among the tents stood a platoon of young Bedouins wearing French army uniforms. They held rifles of three or four different types, with cartridge belts about their chests. The old sheik greeted us pleasantly and pronounced the traditional Arab blessings. Yigal inspected the strange, extraordinary formation and then we entered the sheik's tent for a bit of conversation about the difficulty of the times, the problems of farming and the weather. Once it seemed to us that we'd fulfilled the obligations of courtesy, Yigal guided the conversation toward a more practical course. He told the sheik that his superior had heard of their willingness to join our forces, and therefore he, Yigal, had been sent to meet him in order to work things out. Before he'd finished, the sheik interrupted him in a tone of admonishment: 'O! Eegel my son (that was the way the Arabs of the Tavor region pronounced his name), you can't fool an old man like me. I knew your grandfather, your mother's father, the late Alter Shwartz who was one of the old-timers in Rosh-Pina; I've known your father for the past seventy-five years. You're the Jewish commander and it's because I trust you that I'm ready to link the destiny of my tribe with yours.' " *

In truth, Papa was well known among the Arabs of the Galilee ever since the time he had tried to make a home in Machanaim.

◈ ◈

My father was a stickler about all matters pertaining to the defense of Jewish honor, life and property, which were sometimes one and the same, but he was just as eager to find ways of establishing good relations with the local Arabs. I remember the period following the departure of my big brothers from the farm. My father was already growing old while I was not yet mature enough to undertake the more arduous farm tasks. Like all the farmers, we employed Arab laborers on our farm. Our relations with them were out of the ordinary as such things went.

In the Hebrew of that period such laborers were called tenant farmers. We preferred the Arab term: *charat*. There was a *charat* family which resided permanently in one of the buildings in our yard. In exchange for their work they received a part of the harvest. Good relations sprang up between our families, who lived in the same yard and came into contact every hour of the day.

During the summer breaks, Papa sometimes used to send me off for a week or two, on a vacation at the home of one of his Arab friends. Generally this was at Abu-Ibrahim's place in the village of Ein-Maahal, near Nazareth. Abu-Ibrahim's full name was Abdallah Chabib-Allah. On my return home I would be accompanied by

* Yerucham Cohen, *By the Light of Day and Darkness* (Amikam Publishers), pp. 134–35.

Ibrahim, Abu-Ibrahim's son, and sometimes by another Arab my age as well, in order to spend a week or two at our place. Abdallah Chabib-Allah passed away a few years ago, but to this day we have maintained warm relations with his family. From the time my father died till his own death, Abu-Ibrahim considered himself my guardian. Whenever I turned up in his house his wife would go to some trouble to feed me and see about my needs as if I were her own son. Life's accidents, as they say—the Arab riots, my departure from Kefar Tavor, the war—kept me far removed from Abu-Ibrahim's family and the rest of my Arab friends in Ein-Maahal for many years. Our relations were renewed under extraordinary circumstances.

During the fifth term of the Knesset I was selected for a ministerial post in the government. One of my first official visits was in Nazareth, which I considered the capital city of my childhood. The mayor at that time, Sif-Adin Zoabi, held a warm, elegant reception for me, and then, as I was about to enter the hall, the mayor said:

"I have a surprise for you."

"What is it?"

But instead of answering he asked me to accompany him to a room adjoining the reception hall.

One of the city employees opened the door for us; I entered and came face to face with an old Arab. Although fifteen years had passed since I'd last seen him, I recognized him at once: Abdallah Chabib-Allah, whom we had affectionately nicknamed Abduni. We fell into each other's arms, exchanged kisses and began reminiscing about those distant days. He asked how Papa was, and my sister and brothers, enumerating them each by name. Then and there we determined that I would arrange for a meeting between our two families. He was very eager to see Papa, who by then had already moved to Ginosar. Before I could complete the arrangements for the long-awaited reunion—we had intended to hold it in Abdallah's village—my father passed away. Among the mourners who participated in his funeral was Abduni.

◈ ◈

He was a tall man with broad shoulders, my late father, with blue eyes and black, kinky hair. However, his little beard was blond. This rare color combination was striking to see. He was a tough customer, very strict about everything pertaining to work, punctuality and language. He was known for his honesty and his passion for order and cleanliness. At times, on account of a single grain stalk that had fallen from the wagon, he would raise his voice to us—and not because of the importance he attached to the stalk.

"Those who never saw my father go out in the dark and return late at night from his work in the fields, or pick up a grain stalk that fell from the loaded wagon on the way to the grain shed," my brother Mordechai was to say, "have never seen the love of a farmer for his work. . . . His affectionate caress was granted to ears of grain and delicate flowers alike. He also rewarded us, his children, with the pleasure of duty, and in the harvest season the whole family would go out to work, with the exception of our mother, who remained at home to fix our provisions. We cut the grain and gathered it, picked the chickpeas and sesame. The sowing of the legumes was also done by "independent labor," without that term being used. Most of the tasks in the field, from plowing to harvesting, were done by us, and in the evenings he would require the tired children to attend evening classes (which were organized by the school principal, Antavi) to make up the schoolwork they'd missed. . . . In his love for the land, it was as if my father was competing, so to speak, with the Creator of the World." *

* *Fifty Years of Settlement in the Lower Galilae*, page 207.

While my father plowed the earth in the way of a man with a maiden, as for the tending of livestock, he left that to his wife and sons or to the hired laborers, Arabs and Jews, while he dedicated himself to the conquest of the soil, the grain fields and orchards. He put an infinite amount of labor into the uprooting of rocks and the clearing of his lands, removing little stones and weeds and bushes from his numerous scattered plots. As luck would have it, the lands having been allocated by lot, the field he had won was big and rocky. Day after day, with crowbar and sledgehammer, he extracted the basalt stones from that rocky ground till it became one of the most fertile plots. More than once he told me that just as national sovereignty is based on the nation's ownership of its land, so the farmer's ownership of his land is the basis of his personal freedom, in spite of the floods, droughts, plagues of mice and locusts, and of the human adversaries. Only the land, he would reiterate for my edification, can offer a firm base for the physical existence of man and nation. "It's only the men and nations with land in this world who have an inheritance in this world," he would say.

There was less of the small farmer about him than of the plantation owner, who constantly aspired to enlarge his estate. He hoped to build himself a new house, not inside the village but some distance away, in the midst of the fields. Around such a home, he dreamed, his sons would erect houses of their own. They and all his descendants as well, his grandchildren and great-grandchildren, would not only be attached to the labors of the soil but also bound by their own destiny, love and lives to the village whose land he had joined in an everlasting bond, Kefar Tavor. That was his dream of dreams.

Chapter 8

BOTH IN appearance and manner my mother was a delicate woman, and even though I was only six years old when she passed away I remember her as if we had parted only yesterday: her features, the quiet, modest way she had of speaking, and her devoted, loving attentions to her husband and children. Her good nature was the subject of legends among Jews and Arabs alike. She was a kind of emblem of righteousness, one of the real saints, performing her acts of charity in secret, watching over her women friends when they were ill and taking care of her family and relatives with endless devotion. Her delicate shoulders bore the responsibility for the many chores to be done in the house and yard. She gave everything to others, leaving nothing for herself. She was a devout woman, my mother, observant of all the religious commandments, and she loved and adored my father. Though strictly observant herself, she never tried to force her opinions or way of life on my father, who was a freethinker, or on her daughter and sons, who adhered to their father's view.

Mama was the family treasurer. Even the local Arab women used to deposit their money with her. She was the first to rise in the morning, and as we had no alarm clock her awakening was our sign that it was time to get up. In spite of the sizable family in her charge, she always found time to take care of each of us individually, as if he were her only child. Mama's appearance on Sabbath Eves is one of my earliest memories. It was the weekly focal point for the whole family seated about the big table with the candles burning in their silver candlesticks, the Sabbath bread covered with a white, embroidered napkin and the room perfectly clean and sparkling, emitting a fragrance which one never breathed on weekdays.

She was a beautiful woman, my mother. To this day I remember her delicate, longish features, the sweep of her black hair, her dark, deep eyes and the soft touch of her hand. As the youngest child, it was only natural that I was her pet. She had a profound effect on our home, extending her influence by means of her quiet ways and the warmth and love which she radiated everywhere.

On going outside, she would gather up her hair in a shawl of exquisite, bluish silk, called a *yazme.* Her figure was slender and I remember her wearing a "maxi" skirt, tight about her narrow waist and dropping to her ankles. She wore high-necked blouses with long sleeves that were buttoned at the wrist.

One Friday, after completing her preparations for the Sabbath, she sat down and suddenly collapsed. The doctors were hurriedly summoned to her bedside, but they were powerless to save her. For a week she lay ill, paralyzed, unable to speak. The farmers' wives came and went, sitting beside her bed at night. The voices in the house were lowered without my knowing why. Everyone walked on tiptoe. After all, I was only six. But I remember how my father came in all of a sudden, took me in his arms and carried me to the room where she lay. He hadn't prepared me for that meeting with her, which was to be a farewell. I didn't understand what was going on, but the silence of my relatives who stood about the bed said everything. My father held me over her and I kissed her on the forehead.

If my memory hasn't deceived me, she looked at me too, and her eyes suddenly lit up in her effort to make an impossible smile.

Eliav tells about it in his book:

"The funeral took place that very afternoon in Kefar Tavor, a large procession including relatives, the people of the village and nearby settlements, and some of the local Arabs as well. She was laid to rest in the village cemetery. 'A very righteous woman has departed from us'—so she was eulogized by the head of the burial society, Mr. Dov Hershkovitz of blessed memory. As the grave was covered over Papa lamented her: 'I remember the devotion of your youth, your love as a bride, how you followed me in the wilderness, in the hard life of our village.' "

On her marble tombstone my father ordered that the following be inscribed:

In the shadow of God's refuge may she rest
The most excellent of women
Humanity's glory
MRS. CHAYAH ETIL PAICOVITCH
The daughter of Rabbi Shalom Dov Shwartz
Departed this life on the Fifteenth of Kislev, 5685
In her forty-ninth year

We went back to the home whose rooms were suddenly vacated. Many people came to console us, mostly in silence, occasionally with words. For a very long time after her decease, the villagers and the local Arabs, friends and relatives kept extolling her, and it was plain to see that they spoke not out of politeness but in order to give some expression to the residue of love which she had left in the depths of their hearts.

◈ ◈

As I've said, I was six years old when my mother died and she hadn't had a chance to contribute very much to my upbringing, nor had I to enjoy her motherly attentions. That was a transitional period for me, in which I graduated from kindergarten to the first grade, and the task of replacing my mother was voluntarily undertaken by my only sister, Devorah. Of all the family, only she and I had been born in Kefar Tavor. My brothers had been born in Rosh-Pina, before my parents moved. Devorah was named after the Biblical prophetess in whom my parents took a personal pride, as it were, since they had come to settle in the area which had been the scene of her exploits and the inspiration for her song and prophecy. When my mother passed away Devorah was fourteen years old, in the eighth grade of our elementary school. The circumstances required her to leave school in order to fulfill her duties as a substitute housewife. For a few years she was not only a sister to me but something of a mother as well. Apparently she had inherited a good deal from Mama, considering her good nature and loving attention. But her strictness was acquired from Papa. At any rate, from then on I was treated not only as the youngest son but as an orphan too, and Devorah did all she could to make things easier for me. Her care for me was even exaggerated, but if I managed to receive the required amount of vitamins and proper food, and if I remained healthy during the difficult years following my mother's death, I have Devorah to thank. Having advanced to the eighth grade, she displayed a great interest in my studies and helped me a lot during my first years in school. She was especially good at writing compositions. Whenever I sat down and racked my brains to write something about a book I'd read or record my impressions of a hike, she would sit beside me and offer her advice. It was through her, even more than my teachers, that I acquired the basic concepts of how to approach a subject, analyze it and put it into words. If I was occasionally awarded a good mark in composition, I owe not a little of my thanks for that to

Devorah as well. To this day it's a wonder to me how that woman managed to attain such an estimable level of education, by tremendous efforts of independent study and reading after having neglected, for my sake, the pursuit of her studies in our Galilean grade school. I know it wasn't for me that she went on studying but for herself and the development of her own personality. Nevertheless, I'm grateful to her for that as well, since she unburdened my conscience of all feelings of guilt in her regard. Devorah was a lover of books from childhood, and she encouraged me to read too. Under her influence I began reading and have Devorah to thank for my finest hours in the company of books.

◈ ◈

In our big family, I had a lot of time for myself during Mama's lifetime, and even more so after her departure. My father and brothers were busy on the farm, and though Devorah was strict with me, particularly regarding my food, which she insisted that I receive on time, the heavy burden of the household which she had assumed did not allow her to keep me constantly within sight. I liked to see what was going on outside, as formerly, and from then on I also rambled in the yard a lot, getting to know our animals and running around in the secluded corners of the village and its vicinity. In our home, as in the other homes of our small village, there were no toys to be had. Nature, the yard and all it contained, the fields and the vineyards—they were our playgrounds. We made up for what was lacking in reality by our rich imagination and ingenuity. Like most of the world's children, we too played hopscotch and jacks and especially hide-and-seek, seeing that we had no shortage of places to hide. We constructed railroad trains out of old irons that had gone out of use, the biggest of them serving as the locomotive. We used to load the "freight cars" with prickly pears, and at the end of the "long, exhausting journey," when the train finally arrived at its destination, we would unload it and dine to our heart's content. For many days afterwards our hands and mouths would be full of the little thorns of our prickly, tasty "freight."

Another game which we all loved in the winter was called *dudis:* the player had to take an iron rod and throw it so that it sank into the damp ground; the next boy had to do the same—throw his rod and sink it into the ground—but he would win only if in so doing he managed to knock the first rod over.

This is the place to mention the kindergarten teacher's name, which was that of the kindergarten itself: Rachel Noiman. With her we took our first hikes about the village and its vicinity; by means of the shows she staged, we made our acquaintance with the theatrical world. The same can be said for music, dance, choral singing and much more. She had a hand in everything. Having mentioned the theatre, I might add that we sometimes went to Afula or Tiberias to see a show put on by some professional company which happened to be in town. Such trips were very exciting, our holiday clothes adding to the holiday spirit which filled us even before we boarded the wagon which was to take us to the show. The plays I remember most are *The Dybbuk* as staged by "Habima," which I went to see with my father, and *Yaakov and Rachel*, as presented by the "Ohel" company.

If I haven't so far, now is the time to mention our teenage dances which were held in the village clubhouse. To the music of the flute and, more frequently, the harmonica, we would take our partners, and even I, your servant, was among the musicians (on the harmonica) and dancers. Music was heard in our village at every wedding and national event. On such occasions we used to dance the *Rondo*, a dance which went on for hours with the leading couple drawing the entire population behind them in pairs with their arms linked, young and old alike.

◈ ◈

My father considered carelessness a particularly grievous sin which entailed a heavy punishment. One time he was required to spend two days on business in Tiberias. Before leaving he entrusted me with a simple enough chore: to take care of feeding and watering the chicks. Naturally I was a pretty responsible boy, but that time I just forgot to fill the chicks' trough with water. It was extremely hot that day, but it was only after returning home towards evening that I remembered the chicks and ran to the henhouse. My heart sank: the chicks were dead, all of them. So great was my alarm that I rushed to fill the trough. Papa returned and found on the one hand a trough full of water and, on the other, dead chicks. When he went to the henhouse I declined to accompany him but to no avail—in the distance I heard his voice calling me out, and from his tone I knew what was in store for me.

"Why didn't you water the chicks?" Papa's expression was very severe and there was an unmistakable threat in his eyes.

I was afraid to tell the truth but had no wish to lie, so I said: "But the trough is full of water, just look!"

"If it was any less full," he replied, "I'd believe you really did water them in time and the chicks drank a little." And at once, even before he'd finished his sentence, his hand swung up to slap me. I knew he was right and I had that slap coming to me, but some instinct of self-defense made me shrink back. Papa's hand slapped the empty air and this angered him all the more. He saw my evasion as a sign of rebellion and disobedience, since an obedient son had to be ready to take his punishment and accept even a slap on the cheek. But I, having begun the revolt, resolved to keep on: I simply picked up my heels and disappeared. I knew it couldn't end just like that, and therefore I didn't return home to sleep that night. It was a warm summer night, so I wasn't obliged to look for a place to sleep. Fortunately for me, my brother Zvi, who had already moved to Netanyah by then, was visiting us that day. Naturally, Papa told him what had happened and worriedly added that he didn't know where the "kid" had gone off to. Zvi went out to look for me and around midnight he found me dozing in the vineyard. Thanks to Zvi's custody and Papa's anxiety, I was spared retribution on my return.

Above all, he was a stickler for veracity. To try to deceive him or lie was the most severe offense. Like every father, if not more so, he wanted me to excel in school, more than I actually did, even though I was considered a good student. He insisted that I finish my homework punctually and would stand for no vague answers from me, no guessing. "You don't know—don't answer," he would say; "answer only when you know."

Two or three times a week he would ask me what we'd learned, listening to my explanations, questioning me. That didn't satisfy him, and he frequently consulted with my teachers. At times the teachers would go so far as to visit him at home in order to report on my progress. I was happy to be in a small class, only six students all in all, four boys and two girls. Naturally, in a class of that size we had the supreme advantage of individual attention, but the reason for the small classes was not so happy: the adults of the second generation were moving out of the village, and the enrollment in our school was decreasing from one year to the next. Concern for the future of their labors troubled the founding fathers, and my father was no exception.

His absorption with my studies also entailed strict obligations. His method of education involved the use of constraint, which prompted the father not to spare the rod. I was lucky enough to be on the receiving end less than my big brothers had been, because I was the youngest and also his final hope, seeing that at the time under discussion no one remained at home with him but me, and hence he did all he could to ensure that I would stay on.

I've mentioned our school. Now is the time to speak the praises of my teachers. The truth is that I had fine teachers and have fond memories of each of them: Meiri, Lever and Nafcha, who taught us grammar, literature and arithmetic, geometry and arts-and-crafts; Ephraim Derech, who opened the doors of the *Mishnah* for us. As he taught us its tractates, he tried to instill us with a sense of the period in which it was created, stressing its function in the popular education of those days. I have profoundly affectionate memories of Moshe Grinker, my teacher from Yesud-Hamaalah, who imbued us with a powerful love for the Bible and the Biblical land. He used to guide us through the great expanses of the north, and under his direction they became the expanses of Jewish history; the Bible wasn't a mystical work as he taught it but a book of history, ethics and fine literature, which contained a wealth of geographical and botanical data as well; he would not make do with the accepted commentaries, including that of Rashi, but rather sought authentication in the climate and the farming methods of the Arabs in order to explain the terms we came across in our reading. The *Mishnah* and selected chapters of the *Talmud* were also taught with emphasis on their relation to the living, tangible aspect of the country and the tillers of the soil. It was Ephraim Derech who led our way through the secrets of the Middle Ages, the period of the Crusader kingdom in Israel, the Moslem-Christian wars and much more.

Grinker tried to give us an idea of the difference in the relations between Judaism and Christianity on the one hand, and Islam on the other. As he saw it, between Judaism and Christianity there exists an everlasting enmity never to be bridged, owing to their controversy regarding the Messiah. The Christian religion, according to him, is hostile to Judaism, and he found support for his view in the Spanish Inquisition, the Crusades and the blood libels. It was apparently under his influence that I behaved as I did in Nazareth upon confronting the churches and crucifixes. My teacher pinned his hopes on the understanding which was to be reached between Judaism and Islam, and he demonstrated the possibility of such an achievement by referring to the Golden Age of Jewish-Arab relations in Medieval Spain and before that in Arabia. He regarded the land of Israel as an inseparable part of the Orient, surrounded by traditional Moslem culture. He believed in the possibility of mutual understanding between Jews and Arabs and never lost hope for the flowering of Jewish settlement in this part of the world. It is interesting to note that Papa, whose scars were evidence of his conflicts with the Arabs, agreed with those views. My teachers had never heard of extracurricular education but that was exactly what they introduced, stressing its importance. They managed to make of our little school not only a seat of learning but also an alert, lively social institution offering athletic and cultural activities and also debates, frequently waged with a passion, on the national and popular issues which occupied public opinion in the country at that time. The school contained a relatively ample library, and the teachers encouraged students and adults alike to read.

Chapter 9

PAPA NEVER completed his formal education. He had a few years of instruction in the *cheder*, no more, but he was naturally gifted with a high intelligence and used to read a great deal, in Yiddish, Hebrew and Russian. For my benefit, he would regularly translate poems, fables and proverbs from Russian to Hebrew, sometimes with the book in front of him but generally from the far reaches of his memory. Even if I couldn't see whether he was holding a book or newspaper in his hands, I could tell when he was reading, since he habitually accompanied his reading with a kind of hummed chant, prolonged and almost inaudible, in the manner of the rabbinical students when studying a page of the *Talmud*. His favorite place for reading was the front porch, which was covered by climbing grape vines. His favorite authors were Mapu, Smolenskin, Berdichevsky and I. L. Peretz. Brenner seemed overly pessimistic to him, but he admired his cruel intellectual honesty. Berdichevsky's name was the cause of a considerable insult to me, and many days passed before I got over it. It happened when as a child I tried to pronounce his name and came out with something like Birdy-che-vis-ky. . . . Papa and my big brothers burst out laughing and I ran out of the house in humiliation. No matter how much they tried to placate me, I wouldn't be placated. The humiliation had been too painful.

A particular favorite of his was Yalag. With much eagerness, he would quote passages for us from the dispute between Zedekiah and Jeremiah, stressing Zedekiah's argument, as conceived by the poet, in favor of practical labor as opposed to a Biblical ivory tower. In the same vein I remember Yalag's poem about the Jewish wagoner whose wagon was stuck in the mud; all at once he heard the prophet Elijah instructing him to extricate the wagon by his own efforts. Such poems were meaningful to Papa, since he regarded them as an affirmation of his own revolt against his father and of his subsequent way of life, that of the farmer and protector of his ancestral land. Here it must be added that he himself used to compose occasional verses on current affairs, reading them at family gatherings and sometimes even publishing them in the local paper in Kibbutz Gennosar, to which he moved in his last years.

Papa did not read to himself alone. I still have a vague recollection of how as a little boy, when my mother was still living, I used to roll around at her feet or those of one of the women next door who had gathered at our place, in the early evening, in order to attend a reading session of Papa's. The reading was actually a translation, mostly from Yiddish, with no lack of dramatic expression. For example, arriving at a dialogue he would act out the characters, presenting each of them in a different tone of voice. Needless to say, I no longer remember the content of the stories or articles he chose to read. But the voice, Papa's voice as he read, is still fresh in my mind. Sometimes on those literary evenings my mother would hold me in her lap, and sometimes I would curl up in a corner and listen, not to the words but to Papa's enchanting, melodious voice.

Papa was somewhat taciturn, an individualist, but he was no recluse, a fact borne out by our home, which was always open to neighbors and guests who had stopped off for the night or just a chat and a cup of coffee. Although his life was centered about his home and farm and he had a plantation owner's mentality, he did a good deal of thinking about the public affairs of his village and the nationwide Jewish community. For me, his youngest son, he also used to expound his views on such matters. In this connection I remember his rather unorthodox position regarding the Judean settlements, which was what we then called the citrus growing villages in the center and south of the country. The problem had arisen as a result of the discussions then held on the establishment of a national farmers' association. The Galilean settlements were in a more difficult situation than were their Judean counterparts, and therefore many Galileans supposed that pairing off the Galilean and Judean settlements in a general farmers' union would be like marrying a poor groom to a rich bride. "What," the Galileans claimed, "do we have to do with the citrus barons in Petach-Tikvah and Rechovot? We're wheat farmers and we need an association of our own to watch out for our own interests, not the Judean orange growers'."

Papa, who had never been envious of anyone else's achievements, replied to his zealous colleagues in the words of a Russian proverb: "Wherever you are not is always a nice spot." He was fond of chance remarks, proverbs and fables, and they were his means of getting to the heart of the matter in every dispute.

After the farmers of Kefar Tavor had lost hope for their almond groves, which were greatly damaged by the capnodis larva, they coveted the highly profitable citrus groves. However, their black, heavy soil was rather unsuitable for orange trees, and water was also scarce. Hence they decided to try to find new sources of water by drilling, and then plant grapefruit instead of oranges. But even before the water was discovered the farmers hastily put in nurseries of *chush-hash* trees, on which the grapefruits could be grafted. "If we do find water," they said, "we won't have to waste a year." I too was among the hasty ones and Papa, though skeptical of the citrus boom, did nothing to stop me. He made two points, one correct and the other not quite so. First of all, he argued, who can promise us that the drillings are going to be a success? And the truth is that to this day no great amount of water has been discovered in our parts. Secondly, there's no sense in growing grapefruit. It's different with oranges, they're very much in demand on the English market, anyone can peel an orange and eat it, but grapefruit are bitter—you have to eat them with a silver spoon and they're only meant for the lords and the rich men's market. You can't count on customers like that, he declared.

◈ ◈

One by one the fledglings left Papa's nest to find their own treetops. By the time my sister came of age, of all our large family in Kefar Tavor there remained only the three of us: Papa, my sister and me. My four brothers traveled far to build homes of their own, and our house in the village suddenly became very big, too much so. Moshe, the eldest, moved to Haifa, where he lived to the very last. He was the glory of our family and a source of pride to Papa at home and also during his service as an officer in the Turkish army, and later when he won a job with the railroad company and was the first senior Jewish official on its directorate, becoming, upon the establishment of the state, the director of Israeli railroads. He was one of the few to be awarded the British M.B.E. decoration

(Member of the Order of the British Empire). It's hard to believe he would have received such an honor if they had known about his underground activities in the *Hagana.* Mordechai went off to Binyamina, which is where he built his home and lived all his life. It was he, more than any of us, who seemed to be cast in Papa's mold, and Papa saw Mordechai as his true follower, the plantation farmer whose lands were expansive and diversified. Zvi moved to Netanyah and participated in the founding of that lovely town of citrus groves. Eliav also made his home in Haifa and was closer to our mother than the rest of us in manner and appearance. To the very last he played the role of the family lodestone, uniting us all; it was he who constantly concerned himself with keeping the brotherly relations alive, organizing family reunions, reminding us all of birthdays, wedding anniversaries and memorial days for the deceased, and although considered one of the younger children he was the pivot of our clan after our parents' death.

Thus the three of us remained in Kefar Tavor, but not for long. My sister met the right man, fell in love with him, and her marriage obligated her to move to Haifa. When the time came for her to leave the village, she asked to take me along with her—and my father assented—so that she could continue rearing me and I could attend the distinguished *Reali* high school. There were two reasons for my father's agreement: first of all, he had resolved not to remarry and hence was rather concerned that it would be more than he could manage to rear me, in the most basic sense of the word; he knew the role my sister had assumed in my life, that of both mother and friend, and therefore believed that under her devoted tutelage I would grow up to be a healthy man; secondly, he greatly wished to see me acquire what they called a good education, and the chance of my being admitted to the *Reali* school in Haifa delighted him, although he was very much afraid that the school would change my mind about village life, a way of life which he regarded as vital and unparalleled. Papa and my sister reached a mutual agreement, but things turned out differently, because of me. I simply refused to conform to their plan, for two reasons: I didn't want Papa to remain alone at home, and secondly I was unwilling to leave Kefar Tavor; too many things tied me to the place of my birth. It was a long, wearisome argument between my sister and me, with the occasional intervention of Papa, who declined to take an active part, though his presence was definitely felt. Perhaps my stubbornness secretly pleased him, though from time to time he did try to talk me into accepting Devorah's proposal. I had but one firm answer: "I'm staying with Papa."

Devorah left, and the house was even more empty and large. Of all our sizable, energetic family only the two of us remained in Kefar Tavor, the eldest and the youngest, charged with the responsibility of farming our vast fields and keeping up our considerably augmented barnyard. Papa, a real man if there ever was one, took it upon himself to be a mother as well, and his efforts to fulfill that task in the best possible way knew no bounds. But dreary loneliness prevailed in the rooms, and in his absence I sometimes felt as though I were the only tenant in an abandoned castle.

◈ ◈

The circumstances forced us both to become cooks. Neither of us was very adept in the kitchen, and our recipes were largely the product of our own imagination and ingenuity. Nevertheless, our bachelor cookery had a special, engaging quality about it. Of course the dishes were quite plain and easy to prepare, with a minimum of cooking and a maximum of natural foods. Papa was obsessed with the idea that if a boy ate a lot of broiled liver, he was sure to be healthy. With this conviction he went to the local butcher and reached an agreement with him that whenever the latter slaughtered a calf, lamb or goat, he would save the liver for his little boy, meaning me. And to tell the truth, to this day I know of no greater expert than Papa in preparing that dish. He was so good at broiling it that it was impossible not to give in to temptation and finish it all. A portion that should have lasted us for three and even four days was sometimes polished off (by me, if the truth be told) in a day or two.

I had a different theory about nutrition, which was current among boys my age. It stated that onions and crude olive oil were the foods which bestowed health and potency on a man. It seems to me that my theory was the right one and not Papa's, but from then on I've been living in peace with both of them, onions and liver, which make a good match as far as I'm concerned. But speaking of onions, it wasn't just onions we ate. If I might borrow a few terms from the sphere of art, it wasn't only a matter of content but of form as well, seeing that our preparation of the dish was something of a ritual. In the winter when they grew in the garden, the green onions together with radishes made up the bulk of our salads. In summer when the onions were dry, we ate them only after the most particular, exact preparation: we would take a little, young onion and eat it with bread dipped in the crudest possible olive oil, which had not passed through the final phase of refinement in the primitive olive press and therefore had retained that wonderful, bitter tang of the olive, with its special, tantalizing smell. Sometimes we dipped them in salt before eating them and sometimes, when I happened

to have a lemon or two and some wild sorrel leaves within reach, I'd cut the lemon into tiny slices, mix them with the pieces of onion and the chopped sorrel leaves, top them off with olive oil and the proper amount of salt and paprika and there it was, a salad that could make you its devoted follower for as long as you lived. An omelet containing four or six eggs assured you of perfection.

Sometimes on my return from the fields Papa would surprise me with a boiled chicken and a bowl of steaming soup. As he poured the soup over the rice he would add, laughing, "So when does a farmer get to eat chicken? When he's sick or the chicken is." However, to tell the truth, we ate a lot of them, even when everyone concerned was quite healthy.

◈ ◈

Those three years in which Papa and I lived alone sometimes put me in situations which I doubt many children ever had to face. The new regime obliged me to be more and more self-reliant and this was furthered by Papa's deliberate efforts to train me to be independent, excessively so and surely at too early an age. More than once I had to make my own decisions concerning the management of both farm and household. Little by little he even began asking my advice on matters of consequence, since he no longer considered me just a boy who needed education and care but also a partner who shared the farm and its burdens with him. All at once I found myself, when still quite young, bound to a routine of hard physical labor of a sort almost unknown today. But, to avoid any misunderstanding, I have to make it clear that in spite of those hardships we never felt we were down on our luck. We regarded work as perfectly ordinary, a matter of course, and we accepted it as such—with no self-pity or resentment or complaints against an unjust world. My father must also be credited with the timely purchase of what were then considered modern implements, in order to lighten our burden.

One day Papa decided to make a slight decrease in the

number of cows we kept in our yard. He summoned me and asked: "How would you like to take two pregnant cows to Netanyah, as a gift for your brother? A Negro Bedouin from the neighboring tribe will go along with you."

"Fine," I replied, not concealing my happiness about the adventure in store for me.

In the course of the journey I came to see that the Negro Bedouin was really well acquainted with the paths of the Galilee, the Chefer Valley and the Sharon (Negro families can be found in the Bedouin camps to this day, having arrived in Israel as a result of the slave trade in Africa, in which the Arabs, as is well known, played a significant part). I also saw that although my father had counted on his knowledge of the country's paths, it was otherwise regarding the possible outcome of the journey. He was afraid that if the Bedouin went alone he might sell the cows and then claim that they had been stolen or had fled. Therefore it was my job to keep an eye on the guide.

We set out in the early morning, heading west towards Afula. I rode a horse while the Negro walked behind me. It was the month of Ramadan, a period of daily fasts for the Moslems. I knew the Negro observed the fasts to the letter and therefore offered to change places with him many times, so that he could ride while I went on foot. He had only one answer: "On Ansari's horse no Negro shall ride." All my efforts to convince him came to nothing, so we dragged on at an extremely slow pace, no one being in a hurry, certainly not the cows, who were in their last months of pregnancy. From time to time we would take a break and let the cows munch a bit of grass. By the time we reached the eastern entrance to Wadi Ara, in the vicinity of Megiddo, dusk had already set in. In those days there was a large Bedouin camp of the Arab-Turkeman tribe in that area, and my Bedouin decided that we would spend the night with the head of the tribe. We reached the entrance to a stone building which was completely surrounded by dark tents—that was the period in which not a few Bedouins had already quit their nomadic existence to settle down as farmers. In accordance with the laws of hospitality, we were given a warm, cheerful reception; our cows and my horse were conducted to shelter, with the hosts firmly refusing to let them eat any of the fodder we had with us. Seeing that it was Ramadan, we conformed to custom and spent most of the night dining.

That evening sticks in my mind as one of the most pleasant and interesting times I ever had. True, it wasn't my first visit to a Bedouin camp or an Arab's house, but this time I was the guest of Arabs whom I hadn't known previously, and what was more, this time I was in a camp which even my father had never visited, obviously a guest in my own right. I sat there with my host the whole night, chatting. For quite a while I didn't open my mouth, but little by little I took courage and joined the conversation, which revolved mainly about the problems of farming, with an occasional reference to matters of political import. Someone mentioned Kefar Tavor in a favorable light, praising the industry of its farmers, and once or twice my father's name was heard.

At dawn we took leave of our hosts and I had a good feeling, knowing I'd made new friends. We now made our way slowly through Wadi Ara, which in those days was no more than a winding dirt road parallel to the stream. It was winter and the stream was full of water.

And there was evening and there was morning, a second day. We reached Chadera in twilight. Once inside the settlement, we found ourselves an empty lot where we intended to pass the night under the gray sky. The cows sprawled at rest, the horse was tied to a eucalyptus tree, my friend sat down to watch over the animals and I set out for the center of town in order to stock up on food for the evening. After about half an hour in the grocery I was on my way back to the empty lot when I heard the Bedouin screaming in the distance. I quickened my pace and my heart sank: in front of me, wearing boots and riding pants with a patrolman's wide-brimmed hat on his head stood a hefty Jew who lashed the Arab on the back with his whip. Between one stroke of the whip and the next I heard the big man command the Bedouin to vacate the lot and get out of town. That made my blood boil and I ran up to them, thrust myself in between them and raised my voice to him: "What are you beating him for?" Unruffled by my outcry, he responded by laying down the law: "No Arab is going to spend the night here." "This Arab is a friend of mine and we're going to spend the night here together," I said angrily. "No you aren't, and neither is the Arab, not tonight. Now you just pick up your heels and get out of here fast!"

I looked at the beaten Bedouin and blushed with shame. I remembered how his Arab acquaintances had played host to us in their camp, and now this was our example of Jewish hospitality! I threw a glance at the hefty patrolman and it was clear to me that I'd get the worst of it in a fight.

"Let's go," I said to the Bedouin, "we have to get the cows on their feet."

It wasn't so easy. They were exhausted after two days of walking and we had to "convince" them by turning their tails till it hurt, in order to make them rise. I got on my horse and the journey was resumed. At our rear, as a kind of armed escort, the patrolman tagged along, apparently in order to make sure we put the town far behind.

"Tell me, kid, what's your name?" I suddenly heard his voice at my back.

"None of your business!" I retorted. However, at this

point my friend intervened, apparently having understood the question despite his lack of Hebrew, and he said in Arabic:

"Don't you know who you're driving away? This is Ansari's son! The son of Rim Bakwish from Mascha!"

I don't know if the name of Ansari meant anything to the Jewish patrolman. But the Bakwish (which was the way the Arabs mispronounced "Paicovitch") left no doubts as to whom the Bedouin meant. He ran over to me, grabbed the harness and breathlessly said:

"I didn't know you were Paicovitch's son, forgive me. I know your brother in Binyamina, I know your brother in Netanyah, come home with me, you'll be my guests tonight."

An unbridled feeling took hold of me, of wounded pride or indignation to the point of tears, and I raised the whip in my hand and brought it down on his head with all my meager might. "Get out of here, I'm ashamed of you, I don't want to see your face!" I shouted, much to the Arab's joy, he seeing me whip the Jew who had beaten him a little while before. Our procession lumbered on to the southwest in the direction of Nachal Alexander with the patrolman at our heels, pleading all the way: "Come over to my place, you'll be my guests. I'm sorry, I really am. I didn't know the animals belonged to a Jew. I didn't understand, I didn't know."

I kept on riding and never turned around. He dragged along behind us, muttering apologies till in the end he was tired, it seemed, or just gave up and disappeared into the dark.

Much later, when I tried to figure out the reason for the patrolman's behavior, I came to the conclusion that the attitudes toward hospitality held by the various sectors of our society have fundamental roots. The nomadic Bedouin, camping in the vast wilderness far from the urban centers, regards the whole world as his home; his tent and heart are open to guests, whom he welcomes as he himself expects to be welcomed whenever he happens to arrive in another Bedouin camp. This custom has roots in antiquity, as far back as Abraham, our father, who was renowned for his hospitality. On the other hand the farmer, whose home is his fortress, and quite literally so owing to the threat of nomads and thieves, may have the best of manners and still be suspicious, more strict as a host. Such was the case with the Arab farmer and all the more so with his Jewish counterpart, who had already had his fill of bandits and assailants. Moreover, the Jewish farmer had brought with him the European sense of privacy and introspection.

Meanwhile, our little caravan trudged on in the night, which was very dark. With his extraordinarily keen senses, the Negro Bedouin found his way about like a fox. One thing never stopped bothering him: how and where were we to cross the stream of Nachal Alexander? True, Nachal Alexander isn't the River Jordan, but boats do sail on it and furthermore it was winter then and the rains had turned it into a rushing current. To this day it's a wonder to me how my guide managed to find a ford in the dark, where the water was most shallow. Before long we were on the other side, with both of us and the animals in good shape.

At daybreak we reached my brother's place in Netanyah. Our sudden, unexpected appearance utterly astounded him. Of course he knew that Papa was going to send him two cows as a gift, but he didn't know when and how they would arrive. It never occurred to him that I would be the one to bring them. He looked at me and I at him, and suddenly he embraced me and kissed me warmly and blurted out something about my being a "real sport." Then he shook hands with his old friend from the Arab A-

Zabiach tribe, ran an eye over the cows, rushed us off to the kitchen and immediately following our hurried meal put both of us to bed. If there was anything I wanted most at the time, it was just to sleep.

I don't remember how long I slept, but if I'm not mistaken I went on sleeping all that day and all that night, opening my eyes only the next day at a fairly late hour. To my amazement, I found myself surrounded by a bunch of young people from my village who had been part of the settlement group that founded Netanyah. Their conversation made it clear that they had been there a long time, impatiently waiting for me to wake up, eager to ask me about their relatives and what was going on in the village of their birth. Naturally, I did my best to satisfy them.

I wanted to take a look around Netanyah but it wasn't the easiest thing to do, because my long ride had given rise to an enormous abscess on that part of the body which was in constant friction with the saddle. Walking in the street, I discovered that the story of my trip and especially the part concerning my brush with the patrolman in the old Hebrew settlement had made me some kind of hero for a day in the eyes of my many acquaintances in Netanyah. A few days later I returned home, without any adventures to speak of.

Chapter 10

THE DISAPPOINTMENT of his dream to see the Paicovitch clan firmly established in Kefar Tavor was possibly the greatest tragedy of my father's life. I've already described the erotic aspect of his love for the land, but although he was a romantic type in regard to farming and his attachment to Nature, he was strictly a realist when it came down to everyday matters. Even when reality destroyed his greatest dream, he accepted it with his eyes open and without a trace of bitterness. The first indication that his dream might not come true was the departure of his eldest son, Moshe. He was the best-educated of us, having attended the *Alliance* school in Haifa, a lover of languages which he not only learned but mastered. At the outbreak of the First World War he was drafted into the Turkish army, as I've related, and he rose to an officer's rank. My father, who also served in that army, never got farther than a sergeant's stripes. Apparently my brother's knowledge of languages and his comparative youth were factors in his promotion.

When Jerusalem fell to the British, Moshe was taken prisoner. Though his heart was with the British and not the Turks, he spent two years in a prisoner-of-war camp in Egypt. Papa, who was the head of the village council at the time, repeatedly called on the British Governor in

Tiberias in order to gain the latter's influence in favor of my brother's release. After two years he returned home, as idealistic as ever, a farmer's son who wanted to resume his agricultural tasks. He tried to settle down in the village again, but it soon became apparent to him and my father as well that his place was elsewhere. For some reason he was drawn to Haifa, even though Haifa was still a small town at the time, and one fine day he packed his belongings and left the village. Although Papa had given his consent to Moshe's departure, it hurt him and my mother very much; however, in those days with another four sons and a daughter still at home, he couldn't believe that Moshe's move had put an end to his dream for the clan. But a dream is one thing and reality another. And in reality the farm was incapable of supporting more than a single family.

Before long my second brother, Mordechai, attained maturity. He was faced with a simple choice: he could either receive another farm in Kefar Tavor and incorporate it with our present one if he wished, or he could move on to another place and settle there. In those days there was no chance of receiving additional land in the vicinity of Kefar Tavor; the Arabs refused to sell their plots and the Jewish land had already been allocated down to the last dunam. With no other alternative, and with Papa's consent and even his encouragement, as I was later to learn, Mordechai decided to join the settlement group that founded Binyamina. Thus the first two sons flew the coop.

It was then the turn of the third one, Zvi. He saw no future for himself as an inheritor of part of the farm, and his heart's desire was to build a place of his own. As an active member of the *Benai Binyamin* association he was included among the first group of settlers who were to found Netanyah, in what was to be a citrus belt in the Sharon.

Zvi's departure, unlike that of the first two brothers, is clearly retained in my memory. My father put a sum of money at his disposal for the purchase of a pair of mules, a wagon and work tools. The whole family lent a hand to my brother on his way to independence. Mordechai made a trip from Binyamina to Safed in order to buy him the pair of mules. There was a big to-do at home and not only in our house, since ten of the village youngsters were moving to Netanyah. Late into the night the adults were busy loading the wagons while their younger brothers scampered about in between, skipping over the sacks of fodder with mixed feelings in their hearts, proud of the pioneers who had emerged from their homes and painfully sad because they were leaving. And those were the days of the riots in the country and the red nights which one heard about in the songs of the time.

At dawn the settlers' caravan moved out, escorted by the entire village population, some with a blessing and a prayer and others in envy. Though he had consented to Zvi's step, Papa did not take part in that gathering. With a handshake and without a word he parted from him in the yard and unhurriedly entered the house without looking back. After escorting them for some distance, I returned home. I found Papa sitting in a corner, silent and withdrawn, and it wasn't hard to guess what he was thinking about.

Of all the departures, Eliav's was the most painfully wounding. We were all villagers with an agricultural orientation, but he was the real farmer among us. We were all attached to farm life, but his attachment was the strongest, and he had a particular affinity for the livestock, the mules, oxen and cows with which he maintained an unusual and barely perceptible understanding. I'll never forget how bitterly he wept when Aliza, our best mule, died all of a sudden. He could not overcome his grief, no matter how hard he tried. To console him we looked around for another mule who resembled his beloved and was no less worthy and faithful, but he refused to be comforted. His grief and despair left deep marks on his face. All signs pointed to Eliav, out of all the brothers, as the one who would be the bearer of the farming tradition in our family—and now he left, and not for a new settlement but for the city. To this day I don't know for sure what finished things for him. More than once when reflecting on the matter, I've been inclined to think it was Aliza's death which broke his heart.

On a clear day of winter, when the sun is clearest, there arrived in our village a well-known mule trader from Safed; he set himself up in an empty lot in the middle of the village and displayed his fifteen mules for all to see and buy. The farmers congregated there, either to buy one of the draft animals or just feast their eyes. Papa and I also went over; though doubtful, we hoped we might yet find a mule that resembled the beloved Aliza. Most of the animals were well cared for and looked strong and healthy, but my glance fell on the youngest of them, a female about three years old, brown-colored with a bright, sleek hide, a shapely figure, a thick mane and powerful, expressive eyes. She bore a certain resemblance to Aliza, and at the same time she was quite different. I hoped that when she grew up and was more robust, she might be Aliza's equal. I pointed her out to Papa, but he was afraid that her lack of experience might lead to failure in the test of hard labor. Papa had already turned his back and was ready to go, but I remained where I was, my eyes riveted to her. The clever Arab trader perceived that I'd fallen in love with his animal and decided to take advantage of that fact, in order to convince my skeptical father. "Want to ride her?" the Arab asked me, and before I could reply I found myself mounted on her back. Then the trader addressed my father: "Abu-Eegel, that's a mighty fine boy you've got there!" I did one lap with her, leisurely at first but then moving to a trot and finally a swift gallop in the peculiar style of the mules, their gallop being steadier than a donkey's but more ponderous than a horse's. At the end of the lap I dismounted, patting her neck fondly, my mind made up to try and convince my father to buy her. No great amount of talking was needed. Papa opened his heart and pocket, and after a proper round of bargaining in the Oriental fashion the mule was purchased for twenty-seven pounds, a fabulous sum in those days.

The disappointment came soon enough. A few weeks after buying her we had occasion to see that in spite of her sterility, she being the hybrid offspring of a donkey and mare, she tended to be in heat on certain days of the month. It was an atavistic tendency in her, but quite active. When in heat, she would leave off drawing the wagon and sit down on the shaft, a clear act of masturbation which put our work schedule out of joint. She caused us a lot of trouble and I had to admit that Papa's caution hadn't been in vain, whereas I had based my judgment on appearances alone. I learned that just because something is good it doesn't have to be beautiful, and just because it's beautiful it doesn't have to be of use.

After Aliza's death, we received a letter from Moshe, who was already a senior official of the Mandatory railroad; he wrote to Papa, proposing that Eliav be allowed to try to find himself a place on the railroad staff. Just a trial, he wrote, for one year. In those days there weren't many Jews working on the railroad and Moshe, addressing himself to my father's patriotic sentiments, went into a lengthy explanation of how important it was nationally that more Jews be employed on the railroad, especially since the hostile management disapproved of the hiring of Jews. Once Papa had read the letter, he said to Eliav: "Your big brother wants you to go to work on the railroad. You'll have to decide." His decision was reached, and in order to justify it or soften the blow Eliav replied: "Anyway, there's still Yigal. We'll leave the whole farm to Yigal." Papa wrapped himself in silence. Neither he nor I doubted for a minute that Eliav meant what he said and considered the relinquishment of his rights to the farm an act of generosity, but generosity was one thing and the pain of his departure another.

Eliav always had a special regard for me, as if I were some kind of Heaven-sent foundling. He lavished all the love of his big heart on me. There was a powerful bond between us, and when he left it wasn't only Papa who sensed that something had been severed, shattered forever. He hadn't been gone for long when be bought me a watch for my Bar Mitzvah out of his poor salary and, a while later, a flashy bicycle which he paid for in monthly installments. My joy knew no bounds, and I very much doubt if any boy nowadays can understand what it meant then in Mascha to have a watch and a bicycle.

One way or the other, the dream of Papa's life was no more. At times he would talk to me about it in a sad tone of voice, though he didn't bear any grudges. On the contrary, he was pleased that his sons were getting on well in life, as parents have always been, happy that they had found themselves a good source of income and begun raising families of their own. Now as well, with his dream a thing of the past, his dream of the Kefar Tavor clan, he felt he was the head of a big family, even though it was scattered. It never occurred to him to sell his farm, especially while I still remained, his final hope of establishing the Paicovitch dynasty of farmers on the land he had wedded, the land of Kefar Tavor.

◈ ◈

Everything about him smacked of the farmer, the plantation owner in the traditional sense of the term. He was landed gentry, surely not a socialist. But, strange as it may sound, my father's influence was one of the factors which led me to socialism and particularly to my decision to join a kibbutz. I know at first it's hard to see how that fits in with his clearly patriarchal image, that of a man who would suffer no indignity on his individualistic course. A man who shunned active participation in politics, even though he was a political thinker gifted with a profound patriotic sense which governed his life and actions. Looking back, I have to conclude that perhaps it was his patriotism which brought about the broad transformation in him and his views during the last thirty years of his life. It was his patriotism which led him to rebel against the prolonged and insufferable patronage of PICA.* In fact, my father was the leader of the farmers' revolt against PICA, and he paid for it with not a few material sacrifices. Even I, the youngest son, indirectly became one of his sacrifices, but more on that later.

The story of what happened immediately following the First World War is fairly well known. Baron Rothschild's representative was good enough to make a journey to the Land of Israel, he being Monsieur Franck, whose name alone struck terror in the hearts of Galilean farmers. M. Franck paid an official visit to Kefar Tavor as well. My father was then the head of the local council and in that capacity he presented him with the village's problems and the settlers' demands. When my father had finished his speech, M. Franck said:

"The farmers, sir, have not demonstrated that they are capable of developing their property. We are no idealists and we are only willing to help those who have demonstrated their own ability."

"I'm very sorry," replied my father in a peremptory manner which many of the farmers who attended the

* The Palestine Jewish Colonization Association, established by Baron Edmond de Rothschild—the "father of Jewish settlement."

meeting regarded as overdone, if not actually insolent, "but if you, sir, are no idealist, then you cannot represent the Baron, because the Baron is an idealist; and here in this village only the idealists have remained. Those who were not idealists have already emigrated to America or Australia. With your kind permission, I shall ask the Baron to send us a more idealistic representative."

Surprised, M. Franck listened but made no response. Afterwards he was conducted by my father on a tour of the village. When they reached a blooming almond grove, M. Franck was filled with admiration and asked:

"Ah, I didn't know you had such wonderful trees. Whose orchard is it?"

"It happens to be mine," replied my father.

"My congratulations, sir," said M. Franck. "Come and see me in my office in Haifa."

My father went to his office and presented him with a list of all the farmers and in the next column a list of the loans they requested for development and repairs. Scanning the list, M. Franck saw that my father's name was not included. The Baron's representative understood, and he added my father's name to the list of farmers who were worthy of PICA's support.

This story is no exception in the annals of my father's war against the local PICA officials. He fought them his whole life. The problem was a simple one: the farmers wanted to be released, sooner or later, from PICA's ownership of their land, and they were even willing to redeem their land in easy, reasonable payments; however, the PICA administration was inclined to let things go on as they were, seeing that so long as the land was owned by PICA there was need of its management and if management was needed then officials were too, and the company's staff in Israel knew very well that their principal opponent in Kefar Tavor was my father.

I remember Papa's reaction to the affair of the "contracts." It happened this way: one day a PICA representative acceded to the farmers' request regarding the transfer of their property. When their delegation (of which my father was not a member) arrived at the main office in Haifa in order to receive the eagerly awaited contracts, they were not given actual title deeds but rather agreements which promised the sale sometime in the future. It was a piece of paper that extended the dominion of the officials for another few years. When the delegation returned to the village and gave an account of its achievements to the farmers, my father rose and exposed the fraud with one brief, cutting sentence. "That's not a contract," he said; "it's a con-trick!" As far as I can remember, that was the only time my father ever publicly made such a pithy and unparliamentary pronouncement.

The PICA officials would not condone my father's war against them, and more than once they found a way to get back at him. One time, as the result of an earthquake, big cracks appeared in our house and in many other houses of the village as well. PICA gave loans to everyone whose house had been cracked, for new building or repair. To everyone, but not to Papa. If it had been a question of minor repairs, he could have paid for them out of his own pocket, but in this case it was necessary to build an entirely new house and that was beyond his means. Moreover, the only way to get a loan was to mortgage the property, which he couldn't do, since the title to his farm was held by PICA, so like it or not we went on living in the house with its big, ugly cracks. Once a friend of his, an orthodox Jew, commented on observing the cracks: "In memory of the destruction of the Temple!" To which my father replied: "In memory of the disgrace of PICA."

It is only fair to point out that the villagers had a kind of patriarchal attachment to the Baron. It's rather doubtful if the Baron intended to set up a feudalistic administration in this country, but there's no doubt that his officials managed to give a feudalistic aspect to his enterprise. The Baron's own intentions need no defense and his contributions to the revival of the country are plain to see; his projects constitute an important link in the history of our return to Zion, and it was not for nothing that he was titled "The Father of Jewish Settlement."

I remember that on my first trip to London in 1949 I met Baron James de Rothschild, and he was able to give me a detailed account of the obstinacies of my father from Kefar Tavor, the wars PICA had waged against my brother in Binyamina and its bitter conflict with my own kibbutz, Ginosar. "Tell me," asked the Baron, jestingly of course, "did your father command you to fight PICA on every possible front?"

Now I have to say something about my own brush with PICA—not at Ginosar, but the one that took place when I was fourteen. I had a diploma from our grade school. Papa wanted me to attend Mikveh Yisrael, the high school favored by the pick of the Galilean teenagers, including Eliav, who lauded it and often told me of the marvelous experiences he'd had there. In those days, boys from the Galilean settlements were accepted by Mikveh Yisrael only on condition that they won a scholarship from PICA. Whether one failed or passed the entrance examination was determined by the school itself, but the decision as to who would be admitted was left to the PICA officials in Haifa. And with those officials Papa, as I've related, was constantly at war. Twice I enrolled as a candidate, twice I was invited to the entrance examinations which were held in Yavniel. Twice, to my great surprise, I managed to pass them and even received a formal report of the results—but both times the PICA officials took advantage of their veto.

Chapter 11

PAPA WOULDN'T say no and he looked around feverishly for a school I could attend. Then a new hope appeared on the nearby horizon: at that time it was decided to open a new agricultural school, Kaduri. The proximity of the new school to Kefar Tavor pleased us both. So when it opened I began my studies there, but in the meantime a year and a half had passed in which I'd helped my father with the upkeep and also the management of the farm. Between seasons, like many youngsters in the village, I worked on construction and land-breaking projects.

There's no doubt that my term in Kaduri marked a turning point for me, as regards both my education and my outlook on life. Papa was well aware of that. He understood that I wouldn't just be getting an education there but also encountering young people, members of the pioneer youth movements who had been brought up on socialism. He greatly hoped I wouldn't be among those who had flown the coop, but by his very willingness to send me to Kaduri he assumed that risk as well, for the sake of my studies which he favored no less.

To Kaduri I brought not a little knowledge and experience, a good base for specialization in the field of modern agriculture. Physical labor was already a natural part of my life; I had a great hunger for knowledge and a mighty thirst for a social life which would be richer and more varied than the one I'd known. The fact is that I was ripe for the change which was about to take place in me. Papa followed my progress but never tried to stop me. That was the calculated risk he ran, as I've said, and he was too smart to overlook the danger of separation. But even if he could he wouldn't have stopped me, since he had no faith in common, ignorant farmers. Even so he kept on hoping that my strong ties to my village and home would bring me back to him and his large, extensive farm, equipped with the knowledge which would enable the both of us to modernize it, in accordance with the chief scientific and agro-mechanical innovations of those days.

The scholastic level at Kaduri was high and not only in the agricultural courses, which I could easily keep up with. I remember Papa's response when I presented him with a list of teachers and the subjects they taught:

Shlomo Tsemach—botany and literature;
Dr. Rozenberg—mathematics, chemistry and physics;
Ben-Dor—biology and poultry farming;
Kam—field crops and . . . football;
Dr. Hirsh—cattle and sheep raising;
Noach Naftolski—vegetable farming;
Glickson—orchards and preserves;
Eilon Verchovski—afforestation and gardening;
Efroni—dairy farming;
Zvi and Yaakov—machine trades, metal- and woodworking.

"That's the kind of new thinking we need in Kefar Tavor, son, considering our water and climate and soil. You'll do it, when you're through studying."

Without meaning to slight any of my other teachers, the first and foremost of them was Shlomo Tsemach, the writer and critic who fascinated us with his lectures and talks on botany and Hebrew and world literature alike. He gave me an insight into worlds of which I had had only a glimpse till then, and it was Shlomo Tsemach in particular, as I've related, who opened my eyes to social and human values and, indirectly, to the youth movements, although he constantly expressed his respect and appreciation for the independent farmers, particularly those in the Galilee. Another turning point for me was brought about by the spirited student body, most of whom were graduates of youth movements and urban high schools, with a minority from the independent villages and the kibbutzim. It was a lively bunch, alert, athletic pioneers who were eager for knowledge and new ways of developing the country and themselves.

It was Shlomo Tsemach who proposed to the students, actually the school's first class, a daring gentlemen's agreement which was to be hailed throughout the country: the teachers wouldn't supervise the tests and the students wouldn't do any copying—the honor system. I'd be lying if I said it was easy to fulfill that obligation, but an agreement is an agreement and we made sure it was kept. One time we caught a student in the act of copying. It was out of the question to turn him in to the administration, but we didn't want to break the agreement either. Afterwards we held a meeting and finally decided to tell Tsemach what had happened and that he should cancel the exam. Tsemach listened without asking who the errant student was. He probably knew that we would refuse to inform on him and it may be that he had his own reasons for refraining to put us to such a test. It was enough for him that we had told him the truth, and then and there, in appreciation of our honesty, he decided not to cancel the exam, even if that meant giving the copier something for nothing. "Don't worry," he added in his characteristic vein, "he still has plenty of exams ahead of him."

Papa admired Shlomo Tsemach and was greatly impressed with my stories about him, his vast, diversified knowledge and his simple, noble behavior. Once acquainted with one another, they used to meet regularly at the crossroads, since Kaduri stood halfway between Kefar Tavor and our distant, northern fields. Once or twice he also dropped in on us at home and it was clear from Papa's expression that this was a man after his own heart. They say excessive modesty is a sign of pride, so I won't deny that my father had reason to be satisfied with his son whenever he met with his teacher. Tsemach's reports on my progress in school were quite flattering to him, particularly since he knew of the difficulties I'd had at the start. It had been a difficult beginning, enough to make one give up. True, there were certain advantages in my favor, such as my practical knowledge of agricultural work and my familiarity with the surrounding area and its Arab population, but even so the knowledge gap between me, the graduate of a grammar school in a remote village, and my classmates, who had studied in city high schools, was so wide and profound that in the beginning I almost gave up hope of ever bridging it. However, little by little, and not without the "vigilant perseverance" that those days called for, I became an equal among equals, and in a comparatively short time I even gained a slight advantage, that of the local resident, the native. My classmates nicknamed me Gebeli, in other words "mountain man." The name pleased Papa just as he came to like his "Ansari," which had irritated him at first.

It was at Kaduri that I had my first taste of public affairs. To my great surprise, I was elected to the student council, which had three members out of the twenty-six students in Class One. I was quite flattered by the elections, which took place without any campaigning on my part. Altusha's prophency had come true. The story went this way: when I was born my weight was less than normal. My mother, like mothers the world over, was out of her mind with concern. Her good friend, Altusha Goldman, tried to comfort her and among the honors she conferred on me she said to my mother: "Don't worry, Chayeh, you'll see, this baby is going to be the head of the village council one day." I never did get to be the head of the village council in Mascha, but I was the head of the student council in Kaduri.

◈ ◈

My store of praises is too poor to express what Kaduri was to me and not only to me, to all of us. The teachers, the methods of instruction and dormitory life, the practical work in the branches of modern agriculture, the responsibility for the upkeep of a thriving, developing farm, the concentrated social life with its wealth of youthful pleasures and serious concerns alike, the acceptance of all students as individuals—these made for an educational, fortifying environment. Kaduri was more than just an institution of learning; it was actually a settlement in every respect, rather an isolated one, and in spite of the Mandatory government's aid it was obliged to support itself and defend its lands.

The riots of 1936–1939 cast a heavy shadow over the Jewish community. All over the country and particularly in the Galilee, security was deteriorating from day to day. We proceeded with our studies and work as usual, but the air was filled with the smell of burning fields and the murdered victims' blood. One day in the summer of 1936, I looked out the window in my room at school and noticed a herd of the Bedouins' cattle in a wheat field that belonged to Kefar Tavor. Without stopping to think I alerted some students and two fellow villagers who worked in the school; we broke into Kaduri's storeroom, grabbed some new pick handles which could be used as clubs and dashed out. We ran more than a kilometer, steadily increasing our speed till we reached the field, breathing fiercely. Startled, the herdsmen deserted their herd and fled for their lives. After withdrawing to a safe distance, they stopped and began calling for help, in accordance with the rules of their traditional *fazah*. We were busy driving the herd over to a corner of the field, northeast of the school, when we spotted a horde of Bedouins descending from the hills. It was obvious that they'd soon surround us and cut off our retreat. Since we'd completed our mission—the removal of the herd—and the Arabs had the advantage of hundreds to our few, I ordered a retreat, making a beeline for the school fence. A few of the more agile Bedouins caught up with us and a stick fight developed, a hand-to-hand tussle in the course of which my left shoulder blade was dislocated. We kept retreating, violently waving our sticks to support one another. Approaching the fence, we saw that things were lively enough on the other side: the students together with the teachers, including the principal himself, Shlomo Tsemach, were rushing to our aid, armed with two (licensed) hunting rifles. I yelled at them to fire a few shots in the air but not to hit the Bedouins, who were well within range. A few shots were fired and our pursuers scattered every which way. We jumped over the fence and immediately spread out for defense against the possibility of a renewed attack. This time we had firearms on our side.

We waited for the attack a long time, but it was slow in coming. Policemen appeared instead, British and Arabs, and they arrested us and conducted us with much ceremony to the jail in Tiberias, for questioning. The charge was assault and battery against peaceful Arabs. Tsemach was quite exasperated with me, angry that I had acted independently, without his permission, and disrupted the relations between the school and its Arab neighbors. Nevertheless, in a talk with my father he chose to point out my courage and commend my wisdom. My courage, for having rushed out to rout the trespassers; my wisdom, since even in a tough spot I warned the ones with the rifles not to hit anybody. Tsemach didn't know that I'd acquired that wisdom from my father, as I've related.

Between the fight and the policemen's arrival some hours passed, and of course I could have found myself a hiding place and avoided arrest, and I would have done so were it not for Papa's insistence that I present myself to the police: "You have to claim that you went out to drive the herd off your father's fields and you wounded the Arabs in self-defense—is that clear?"

"Clear as day," I answered and tried to get used to the idea of an adventure in jail.

After a few days of confinement in the old city wall we were all released on bail, which was paid by our parents, while the reins of justice were put in the trusty hands of the attorney A. Choter-Yishai, from the trial service of the *Hagana.* At the trial itself, my testimony carried weight and even the British judge was obliged to take it into consideration. True to my father's guidance, I repeatedly claimed that I hadn't gone out to do the Arabs any injury but simply to protect Papa's harvest; it wasn't us who had started the fight but them, our neighbors; and if a few of them had been wounded in the fray it was their fault, since we had acted only in self-defense. The British judge, Harvard, listened, jotting down whatever he saw fit on the pages before him, and finally he acquitted us on the grounds of self-defense. The trial, and especially our days in prison, made the skirmish twice as important and inflated our pride. Mine knew no end: Papa had done time in a Turkish jail, actually on two occasions, in Safed and Nazareth; my eldest brother had also been confined for two years in a British prisoner-of-war camp in Egypt; now I too had a taste of the British prison in Tiberias, to whose walls I was to return two years later (1938) as a sergeant in the Jewish Settlement Police, in charge of the mobile patrol. As fate would have it, I was confined in the very same cell. This time I was accused of the murder of the leading Arab fisherman in Tiberias. Of course it was no murder, but the killing had been intentional, and the victim was no righteous innocent, Heaven forbid, but rather the leader of the Arab gangs that smuggled arms from east to west across the Sea of Galilee. Under interrogation I delivered an impassioned speech, the theme of which was: "My honorable interrogators, I and my fellow patrolmen do not deserve imprisonment, but a medal!"

We didn't get our medal, but after a week of imprisonment and interrogation, including the reconstruction of the ambush we had set for the arms-fisher in the mouth of Nachal Amud, on the shore of the Sea of Galilee, the charges against us were completely withdrawn.

◈ ◈

The riots of 1936–1939 left a deep mark on the Jewish community and radically influenced the outlook of the country's inhabitants in general, and especially that of the Galilean farmers. Every round of bloodshed prompted a grave concern for the very existence of our community, but there were also instances of courage and valor which fired the imagination and gave shape to our thoughts and actions. The riots, especially during the 1936–1939 period, demonstrated without a shadow of a doubt that the collective settlements were superior to the independent ones where the protection of life and property was concerned. For example, we learned that distant fields, each of which was cultivated and guarded by its owner alone, meant that Jews had to be spread over an extensive area, leading to almost insurmountable difficulties during guard duty and unnecessary risks of life.

Some people acquired their collective and socialist philosophies by means of the revolutionary movements, under the influence of leaders and theories; I got mine through practical action. Reality took precedence over thought and determined its course. One day, with Papa's encouragement, I mustered fourteen out of the thirty-six farmers in Kefar Tavor—the ones whose fields lay to the north of the present-day Kaduri, in the area whose lands were known by their Arab name, Um-Agabl (the Mother of the Mountains)—and I proposed that we join together in a cooperative, meaning not the abolition of the private ownership of their fields, not a merger, but simply an agreement to cooperate in the cultivation of the fields and take an equal share of their yield, regardless of the individual yield of each plot and the amount of damage done by gangs or fires to one field or another. I know that a proposal of that sort may sound very simple and even obvious today, but at that time, in such an individualistic settlement of solid farmers, each of whom was passionately attached to his own plot of land—and by that I mean no disparagement of them, quite the contrary—such a proposal was considered extremely revolutionary. My proposal astounded the farmers, but they were even more surprised when my father seconded me. I remember the expression on their faces when he took the floor. You could see the question in their eyes: "What? He too, the confirmed individualist, he agrees?"

One meeting followed another, held in a tense, fiery atmosphere—some farmers were in favor, some opposed and others could not make up their minds, as usual. Between one meeting and the next, when my father's back was turned, they used to say, half-seriously, that it seemed the facts of life had forced him to change his ways and opinions. So long as he had five able sons and a daughter at home, he had no use for cooperative labor since he had his own collective—that was the way he himself described it on more than one occasion—a family collective; but now in his old age, when he had no one left on his big farm but his youngest son, it was no wonder that he suddenly adopted strange, socialistic ideas about cooperative fields and maybe even—God forbid—orchards!

Though influenced by our physical circumstances, his philosophy of life was strictly individualistic. Nevertheless, he came to see that in a state of siege, no individual can hold his own alone. In order to justify the change of values which had taken place in his basic philosophy, he adopted the famous saying of Hillel the Elder, using its first clause to express his individualistic outlook—"If I am not for myself, who will be for me?"—while the second clause of the saying confirmed his acceptance of the individual's need of society: "And if I am only for myself, what am I?"

The decision was reached and it was resolved that there would be only a certain degree of cooperation. The participants unanimously decided to cooperate in the cultivation and harvesting of their lands, but the harvest of each one's field would remain his. In the concluding debate Papa said: "Instead of fourteen farmers with fourteen pairs of mules and fourteen plows spreading out on fourteen different plots, we'll all go out to one field, plow it, seed it and cultivate it, and together we'll go on to the next field until we finish seeding them all. That's the way we're going to seed them and that's the way we're going to harvest them and bring the crops in to the grain shed."

That episode also marked a turning point in Papa's views; he began to speak favorably of collective farming, but he used the word "collective," preferring it to the other term, kibbutz. It wasn't that he'd become an advocate of the kibbutz way of life; he went on criticizing it for what he saw as its lack of a farmer's individual attachment to his land and personal motivation, which he considered necessary for increased productivity and yields on the farm; but in general it may be said that he now took a more positive view of that way of life.

At the same time I occasionally stopped off at kibbutzim such as Deganyah-Alef and En-Harod, and on my return home we would discuss our impressions of the similarities and differences between our way of life and that of the kibbutz, and of the people in the kibbutz, many of whom he knew quite well. Among his personal acquaintances were Aharon Tzizling and Shlomo Lavi from En-Harod, Yosef Baratz and Yosef Fein from Deganyah-Alef, Ben-Tzion Yisraeli from Kinneret and Rozenfeld from Deganyah-Bet. He was on friendly terms with the first settlers in Merchavyah and the *Hashomer* patrolmen, many of whom were regular guests in our home. None of those people were strangers to him nor was he to them; he thought highly of them and their work, but even so I have to admit that his warm attitude toward the cooperative way of life was rather a surprise to me.

Naturally, he preferred the independent village to the kibbutz, but being a consistent type who never liked to compromise, he couldn't see anything in the *moshav*, a farming village which was a kind of cross between individualism and collectivism. "Either one way or the other!" he would say, true to his drive for integrity.

◈ ◈

One day a contingent from the *Gordonyah* movement came to work in our village. Its members were put up in some cabins on the outskirts of the village. The pioneers had come for two reasons: to learn the work, and to win themselves jobs by doing better than the Arab tenant farmers. Papa was one of the first to accept two pioneers for work in his fields. I remember them both, especially Zeev, a tall, swarthy young man with a warm heart. I've forgotten the name of the other fellow, the redhead. They were new immigrants just arrived from Poland, with a fine education and a powerful desire to succeed in their work. Their desperate efforts to win jobs for themselves were worthy of admiration, but it wasn't easy to watch them unloading hay from the wagon on a really hot day, with the gnats getting into their ears and sweat pouring down their blazing foreheads. It was quite a pitiful sight. Looking at them, Papa said there wasn't much chance of their sticking it out. And to tell the truth, their efficiency was on a lower level than ours and even the Arab laborers', while their pay was higher, but they made up for the lack of experience with a will of iron.

Through them I gradually grew closer to the rest of their group who were undergoing their apprenticeship in our village. I was drawn to them out of curiosity. But it was also my loneliness, the loneliness of a boy without a mother or a warm home, which led me to their dining hall to have a cup of tea with them, listening to their talk and enjoying their company. I was fascinated by their behavior and, needless to say, their passionate dances, which went on till the wee hours of the night. There was something new, fresh and delightful about the collective life and the way those pioneers lived it. I know now that my introduction to them and their world also had its effect on the formation of my views and future development.

The barriers between the people of Kefar Tavor and the recruits from the labor force weren't removed in a day. The decisive turning point in both Papa's and my attitude toward them came about at the banquet—which was our term for a party in those days—in honor of some settlement's anniversary, Rosh-Pina's perhaps or Kefar Tavor's, I no longer remember, but I do remember that the event was widely celebrated. Everyone in the village took part, as well as people from the nearby settlements who poured into our village, riding their horses or lumbering along in wagons packed with merrymakers. Though they usually kept to themselves in their independent group, the members of the labor force were also invited to the banquet. The annals of Jewish settlement furnished one of the chief attractions of the party and among the principal storytellers—storytellers and not speakers—was my father. I believe I've already said something about the way he had of captivating his listeners with a story. People could sit with him for hours on end listening to his stories, which were always exciting even when they had to do with simple, everyday affairs.

That evening he enlarged on the initial settlement of the first fourteen farmers who had come to establish themselves on the lands of Um-Agabl, on the slopes of the Nazareth mountains north of Kefar Tavor. Though replete with details, his story flowed on freely with a witty charm throughout. When he finished, his listeners applauded him, cheering loudly. Everyone was enthused and especially the members of the labor force, who dreamed of their own settlement. The next day the head of their group appeared in our home, and after lavishing praise and gratitude on Papa for his wonderful story, he asked him to come to the group's cabin and tell them the sequel, about the next period in the history of our village. My father accepted the invitation and I gladly joined him as one of the listeners. That evening, in their meager cabin, I sensed that whatever had stood between us had evaporated, and now things could flow both ways, free of all prejudice; there was some invisible bond between my father and those youngsters. Till then we had regarded the kibbutz as something rather strange, even suspicious, and here we were sitting among them, the ones who aimed to found a new kibbutz, and the invisible barriers which had always stood between us were no more.

◈ ◈

The drive, vigor and staying power which the collective settlements displayed during the riots that swept the country, as well as his close contact with the labor force in our village, gave Papa plenty of food for thought. I don't mean to say that his basic concepts were revolutionized—they remained as they were—but his receptiveness to new ideas and procedures saved him from stagnation. Far be it from him to toe the line and make do with what he had. He was aware of the fact that a farmer's mentality was sometimes equated with ignorance, an analogy which had never enchanted him. Therefore he was constantly concerned that his sons should acquire a proper education, just as he was constantly on the lookout for agro-mechanical innovations which could be used on his farm. I've already mentioned that he was in every sense a plantation owner, but of the new, enlightened kind. Although he was one of the leading voices in our village, he didn't always succeed in winning his contemporaries over to his ideas. Such had been the outcome of his attempts to organize the villagers on a cooperative basis. Now, as no one remained at home with him but me, I became his partner in everything, the burden of the farm and his soul-searching and thinking as well. The things which had started Papa thinking played on my mind too, but they were actually just fragments, premature thoughts, more like questions than clear, definite answers. At times I said to myself that if the cooperative cultivation of the land was really preferable to individual farming, then it followed that the kibbutz was preferable to the cooperative farm, since in spite of the considerable advantages of the latter it had not eliminated inequality among its members, at least insofar as property was concerned; and in that case, I reasoned further, perhaps it was the kibbutz rather than the independent village or "collective fields" which fully answered to the needs of the country and the aspirations of man, who was a social creature in respect of his environment and inclinations alike. One question led to another and all of them together were eventually to bring forth my answer, one which Papa never had in mind and could hardly be pleased with. One way or the other, the seed was planted and he had not a little to do with it.

It was no abstract theory or detached contemplation but rather reality as we perceived it and the questions it raised which determined our way of life; however, a vital role in the formation of my views was played by the books and periodicals which found their way into our home. He was a man of the soil, my father, but also a man of letters. His love for the written word knew no bounds, and in every free hour, even after a day of hard labor, I found him with a book in his hands. He was a voracious reader of newspapers too, domestic ones and American papers in Yiddish. The newspapers we received had no socialistic tendencies to speak of. Once a week, six issues to a bundle, the *Doar Hayom* would arrive, a daily edited by Itamar Ben-Avi, the son of Eliezer Ben-Yehuda. As far as I can remember, it was lively enough, although I suppose that if I were to go back and take a look at its old pages today I might very well differ with many of the opinions therein. However, at the time that newspaper had a patriotic role to play, in the more elevated sense of the word, since it was basically an educational journal which gave good coverage to the problems of the independent settlements and their farmers. It also provided space for the views of the second generation in the settlements who were organized in the

Benei Binyamin, named for Baron Binyamin de Rothschild. And strange as it may seem, though they tried to extricate themselves from the Baron's officials, the younger farmers never relinquished their warm, sentimental regard for the "Father of Jewish Settlement." This wasn't a distinction which only became clear in the course of time; it existed even then.

If *Doar Hayom* was our daily paper, then our weekly was *Habustanai*, a farmers' journal which maintained a high literary and political level and was edited by Moshe Smilansky, the writer and farmer from Rechovot. As for its philosophy, I felt closer to Smilansky's ideas than to Itamar Ben-Avi's. Smilansky was no nearer to socialism, but he wasn't a stranger to the workers' movement and the desires of the working man.

Our village was small and somewhat isolated and remained so even when connected by highways to Afula and Tiberias, but it possessed a whole world of its own: the library. The best of Hebrew literature and foreign works in Hebrew translation found their way to its collection. Every new book published by Omanut, Masada, Shtibel, Dvir and Mitspeh would automatically arrive in our library. Our love of books and reading was fostered not only at home but also by our teachers, and in this regard they were quite strict with us. In order to make sure we'd done the reading and, even more important, that we'd understood, we were required to write short book reports, a method which succeeded in instilling the love of books in us and also improved our capacity for self-expression, giving us a firm foundation for independent study.

Here and there I also came across various pamphlets and articles by labor leaders in this country and abroad. I must admit that my first encounter with their writings left me cold. The terminology was strange to me and at first I read them without the slightest interest, but little by little the strangeness gave way to understanding, and eventually to rapport.

From time to time, people from the kibbutz movement turned up in our village in order to give lectures on a wide range of subjects. Papa, who was eager for knowledge and liked to test out his views in confrontation with dissimilar ones, never missed a lecture. I generally went along with him, whether in order to listen to his questions and arguments or to swap impressions with him later. One lecture which has stuck in my mind was given by Ben-Tzion Yisraeli from Kinneret, who was not an accomplished speaker but nevertheless won the hearts of his listeners with his frankness and his sense of identification with the way of life he called for, a way of life in whose realization he had played a principal part. Nearly everyone in Kefar Tavor congregated in the modest assembly hall to hear what he had to say. In the course of the lecture he dwelled on the connection between his kibbutz, Kinneret, and our village. He pointed out the things they had in common but did not refrain from analyzing their differences as well. The comparison intrigued me and I pondered over his lecture for many days.

Chapter 12

LIKE MOST village youngsters in those days, I too was drawn to the *Benei Binyamin* movement, which was organized by the second generation of farmers in the older villages. When the movement died out, I took the initiative and with some of my contemporaries I established the Mascha branch of *Hamaccabi Hatsair*. We saw the *Hamaccabi Hatsair* as primarily an athletic and not a political association, and our approach was in harmony with the accepted attitudes in Kefar Tavor. Even so it should be noted that we chose *Hamaccabi Hatsair* and not *Hamaccabi*, because of certain principles held by the former which we hadn't found in the latter. Although we would not join any movement with a definite ideological persuasion, we were no strangers to the trends of the time and our choice of *Hamaccabi Hatsair* was by no means haphazard. Two movements vied for our tender loyalties, *Betar* and *Hanoar Haoved*. However, we took it upon ourselves to set up a branch of *Hamaccabi Hatsair*, which we called *Maccabi Moshe* in honor of Moshe Klimentovski, the youth from Kefar Tavor who fell in battle, as described in a previous chapter. The choice of that name was no accident: we wanted a hero of our own, someone who had lived, worked and fallen on our land.

The branch divided its attentions between athletic

events, which were also held in Tiberias, and "educational activities," as they were then termed in the youth movements. When the central office of *Hamaccabi Hatsair* was informed of the branch we had established in our village, they began sending us the literature published by *Hamaccabi Hatsair* whose ideological tendency, as I've said, was close to that of the settlements, the kibbutz and the workers. Those publications also had their effect on us, making us receptive to the state of mind in the labor movement.

My impasse with *Hamaccabi Hatsair* was reached during one of the conventions held by the *Hamaccabi* movement, the first of them if I'm not mistaken. The convention was held in Tel-Aviv, where at the same time an international conference of *Hamaccabi Hatsair* was going on. That conference marked the first appearance of two parties: the strictly athletic, right-wing party, and the settlement party. During the discussion Yosef Baratz from Deganyah-Alef took the floor and waged a fierce debate with the bourgeois sportsmen, as we then called them. However, I was less affected by what Bertz said than by a seemingly trivial incident, which was nevertheless the determining factor in my future relations with that movement. In the inauguration ceremony of the conference, one of the central committee members from Hamaccabi rose to the stage to speak, an adult. Even before he'd opened his mouth I began to dislike him. He stood there on the stage, a man in his forties, wearing sparkling white trousers with a neat press, a sporty tie and a blue jacket which was adorned with a flashy *Hamaccabi* emblem. He talked about sports, the role sports played, the value of sports and how important they were, but there was something definitely unsportsmanlike in the looks and demeanor of the man. As I've said, he wasn't very young or solidly built: he had a big belly, swollen and drooping, and I have to admit that this was also a factor in my antipathy to him, since I had a different idea of how the leader of a sporting movement should look; however, it wasn't his appearance which caused my disgust and provoked my anger against him and the movement he represented, but something else again, a passage in his speech which really made me clench my fists. After he had began his speech by paying tribute to patriotism with a few clichés, he got down to the point, which was that we youngsters would do well to follow the example of the Black Shirts of the Italian Fascist Party, since they were the very model of patriotism, strict discipline and self-sacrifice for the good of the homeland. "They," he exclaimed, "should be our teachers, and it behooves us to be guided by their shining light. . . ." I didn't hear the rest, since the minute he uttered that sentence I sprang up and dashed out to the fresh air.

I never joined another youth movement, although as a student at Kaduri I spent most of my time in the company of some wonderful fellows from the *Hanoar Haoved* and *Hamachanot Haolim* movements. I was later to join the kibbutz with that group, but in Kaduri itself every time I was asked what I was going to do and where I would go once I finished school, I replied that my place was in Kefar Tavor, I loved my village and was tied to my father's farm. During my freshman year, at least, I was quite firm about that, and the departure, which was not yet a turning point, occurred in my second year, when ideological considerations began competing with my natural sentiments. The social and moral distinction of kibbutz life, the qualitative standard of living, the human equality and mutual support which were upheld in the kibbutz more than in any other form of society, these were my proof that the new order of which the world's reformers throughout the ages had dreamed was not a utopia but rather a tangible reality, taking shape before my very eyes.

From day to day my conviction grew that the kibbutz way was the right one in the Jewish community, the nation and the commonwealth of mankind, and from day to day I was more eager to join it. At the same time I came into closer contact with the older kibbutzim and their young people. We held social functions regularly, with joint activities, dances, hikes, talks; once or twice I also had the chance to attend conventions of the younger independent farmers in the Lower Galilee, and on such occasions we looked for ways of improving our villages. At those conventions I came to see that there was no way we could think of which didn't lead, in the long run, to collectivism. From an ideological standpoint, I was already ripe for a decision, but in the days under discussion the decision had yet to be made.

◈ ◈

The bloody riots in the country became fiercer. At Kaduri, the administration elected to take a recess for a few months and send the students home. Returning, I plunged into work on my father's farm, he having borne the yoke alone till then in the absence of the Arab tenant farmers, who had fled to their villages. From then on I had to divide my time between a full day's work on the farm and full-time service in the defense of the settlement and its fields.

It was 1936, the year in which the foundations were laid for the Jewish Settlement Police. Together with a few other young men from my village, I volunteered for service in that force. We looked a little peculiar in the uniforms and particularly the Circassian fur hats. But our pride and joy was the English rifle which had come into our possession. It was a shining new rifle with a ten-round clip and fifty rounds in reserve in the khaki pouch. In those days we considered it a regular arsenal.

The swearing-in ceremony took place in Afula, and upon returning home proud and happy I hung my new rifle on a hook on the bare wall of the room. Papa looked at me without saying anything, but it was obvious that he was happy for me. He also had a rifle, a German model, but he couldn't hang it on the wall because it was illegal.

All at once he said to me: "Remember that rifle that Moshe brought for Mordechai? The rifle from the Turkish spoils?" The very question made his feeling clear: the Paicovitch history was repeating itself, one brother after another and all of them in Papa's wake, taking arms for defense. Now it was the turn of the youngest son, who was also the youngest member in the local unit of the Settlement Police.

The days were devoted to work on the farm, and the nights to guard duty in the village and its fields. One day in the early afternoon, the alarm was sounded. I took my rifle and hurried to the center of the village. There we were informed that two of our buddies who had been on guard in the fields were under attack, and reinforcements had to be rushed to them. Spontaneously, in disorder, we all dashed off each at his own pace in the direction of Wadi Sharar, about a kilometer and a half south of the village. In the olive grove near the wadi, we prepared ourselves for the battle. I unwittingly recalled that my brother Zvi had been wounded not far from that wadi in 1920, when pursuing the thieves.

We separated into two groups, the first headed by M. Y. Cohen, the village commander, and the second by me. He opened fire to cover me and four of my men, all of them older than I, as we charged the attackers. Under mutual cover, the gang retreated towards the wadi, the famous Wadi Bira, and vanished in the dark of the descending evening. Meanwhile in the village the older people, my father among them, took up positions for defense against a possible attack from the other side. With the battle nearly over, reinforcements reached us from the Afula police. Together with the two guards who had been attacked, we returned to the village, safe and sound and full of satisfaction. The next day we revisited the scene of battle and discovered many bloodstains. Later we were informed that one member of the gang had been killed in that battle and another wounded. Our victory was complete and so was the victors' joy.

From time to time the gangs would set fire to fields where the crops were ripe. As the commander of the local mobile patrol, it was my task to rush with my unit to the distant, burning fields and put out the fire. The fire-fighting operation was quite dangerous, since the flames lit us up as we assaulted them with our pitifully primitive devices, and we made a distinct easy target for the marauders' bullets. Even so, there were only one or two instances in which effective fire was directed at us while we fought the flames. Papa, who took an active part in the settlement's defense, was proud of my exploits but fearful for my safety. That was plain to see, although he did everything he could to restrain his feelings. He would part from me worriedly as I went out on duty, but he never tried to stop me.

The times had changed: not long ago, in the riots of 1929 when I was eleven years old, the village was attacked and Papa took his rifle and ran out to his position. Before leaving the house, he carried me up by ladder to the attic, fitted me out with a sharp axe for self-defense and a supply of food and water, and said: "You stay in the attic till I'm back." In order not to give away my hiding place, he removed the ladder to the yard. That scene was repeated many times. I would stay in the dark attic, trying to guess how the battle was going by the shots. Sometimes

I fell asleep but usually I struggled with my fear till he returned. At dawn he would appear and take me down from the attic. He was happy when I told him I'd had a good sleep and I was happy to see him safe and sound and to hear that the attacks had been repulsed, without my having to use the axe. The very thought that I might have to use it made me shudder. In those nights in the attic I was afraid for his safety and there was no one with me to share my fear; now in 1936, the order was reversed and it was he who remained at home, afraid of what might happen to me.

My buddies and I did what we had to. It never occurred to us that we were making history; we simply acted as required by the circumstances and our need of protection, and thus my surprise was so great when it turned out one day that we had been among the first to go "outside the fences," without anyone having told us to do so, and among the first to carry the battle into the open fields. in the best tactical tradition of those days. Our district commander, Nachum Shadmi (Kramer) from Menachemiyah, who put a great effort and much talent into our training and drilling, was proud of his charges, if one could take his word for it as we, of course, were happy to.

◈ ◈

In the spring of 1937 I first met Yitzhak Sadeh, the man who was to play a vital part in my life. It was a threshing day, blazing hot, and in the absence of the Arab kids, who had all picked up their heels and made for their villages the minute they heard the first shot, I had to turn the sledge by myself in my father's grain shed. It was a boring job which put one's mind to sleep and dulled the senses. You couldn't plunge into it or ever think about it: you just went round and round automatically, like a wheel. But then, as I made another monotonous turn, the youngest son of the village commander ran up to me.

"They want you to come to Papa's house right away," he blurted, breathing heavily; "there's a staff officer here from the *Hagana.*"

I quit threshing and rushed to the commander's house. I was introduced to a tall, broad-shouldered, muscular man, a little on the heavy side and bald with a fatty bump on his forehead. He was dressed in short pants and high green socks, which were the fashion in those days; his shirt, as I remember, was light-colored with the sleeves rolled up, and to complete the dismal picture he wore glasses.

"I want you to meet Yitzhak Sadeh," said my commander; "he's been sent here to organize a mobile field squad."

We shook hands, and I doubt if I managed to hide my confusion and disappointment from the "staff officer." I don't remember his first words, but I have a clear recollection of the deep, rather husky voice in which he explained the purpose of his visit: "The *Hagana* staff has decided to set up a nationwide mobile unit which will be called FOSH—field companies. This force will be under my command. The members of FOSH will be under national jurisdiction and they'll be sent wherever the force is needed. I presume that the volunteers for FOSH from Kefar Tavor will remain in the Galilee. The Galilee needs a defense force. Would you like to volunteer? Do you have any friends who would?"

I've already said that my first impression of the man wasn't especially appealing. As he spoke, I thought to myself: Who is this bald, toothless old man to teach us the art of war, as if we didn't already have a long list of impressive operations to our credit? True, I was fascinated by the idea he had presented, very much so, but not by the man himself; nevertheless, I was quick to respond: "Yes, I'll volunteer. What do I have to do?"

"Assemble some of your buddies this evening and we'll go out on a night exercise." That was the kind of definite answer I liked. I returned to the grain shed to take the mules back to the stable. At home, I told Papa about my curious meeting with the strange man. His name, Yitzhak Sadeh, meant nothing to Papa.

"Did you agree?" asked Papa.

"Yes."

"All right," he said, just as I expected, since he never tried to stand in my way.

Towards evening, at the edge of the village, a small group of young men assembled and Yitzhak Sadeh briefly explained the course of the exercise:

"We'll take the path for the Mugrab village, about four and a half kilometers from here. We'll set an ambush near that village. I hope we'll encounter a gang, either on its way out for action or on its withdrawal. That's all."

His statement was brief, forceful and clear. We were surprised; we had never done anything like this. The tracker was ordered to go first and Yitzhak Sadeh followed him, leading our little column. Since he was nearsighted, his feet didn't miss a single stone on the way, and the noise he made resounded afar in defiance of all the principles of infiltration at night. His way of walking did nothing to enhance his appeal; but it was otherwise regarding the great confidence with which he strode on, a confidence which prompted our trust in the man who strode before us and led us far beyond the usual range of our marches, which had not been so insignificant either. We arrived at a certain place and he ordered us to set up an ambush and secure the flanks. "Just to be on the safe side," he said. Silently, we lay in ambush with a prayer in our heart for the gang to show up, but that night our prayer was not answered. The gang declined to appear. As dawn approached, he ordered us to fire a few volleys in the air, in the direction of the village. We did as he ordered.

"That's all," he said and the little column retraced its steps.

Before daybreak we were already walking down the main street of our settlement, inside the "base"—our home yard. We gathered dry twigs and lit a little campfire, and as we sat there Yitzhak summed up the exercise:

"If we take to the paths and set up ambushes and fire at their bases, whether we encounter them or not, the Arabs won't be the masters of the night any more. We'll cut down on the manpower we need for static defense. If we have the good sense to change our tactics from time to time so that we always have a fresh surprise in store for them, they'll be put on the defensive in order to protect their villages. We won't go in for murder or personal terrorism, but we will force them to watch out for themselves. That's our doctrine in a nutshell."

The doctrine was simple and so were the words: clear, easily understood, practical. Fragmented thoughts which had troubled our heads for a long time were suddenly crystallized. A wonderful feeling took hold of us all and we instinctively knew that this was the man. The initial barriers and misgivings disappeared. Meanwhile we were served warm milk fresh from the cow, milk which had not been boiled, of course, and although the talk was already over we went on sitting about the campfire, the first in which I participated with Yitzhak. Then Papa came up. During the talk I had seen him standing to one side, leaning against a wall and listening.

"Meet my father," I said to Yitzhak.

Yitzhak got up and saluted. Papa shook hands with him

and accepted the salute as if it were only natural. Suddenly he squinted and said in a questioning tone:

"My son Yigal told me your name was Sadeh. I never heard that name, but you look as if I knew you years ago. Wasn't your name Landsberg or Landberg, something like that?"

"Yes, my real name is Landberg," Yitzhak confirmed, "but I'd rather be called Sadeh."

It was time for the company to disband. Yitzhak also said goodbye, got into his car and drove off to enlist more field companies.

Chapter 13

I WENT BACK to Kaduri to complete my course of study. Our deliberations regarding our future were soon to be ended as well. In the opinion of all my classmates, it fell to us to form an independent youth group for the purpose of settlement. Our decision was infused with a special brand of patriotism, since we believed that as graduates of a government agricultural school we had good prospects of receiving a plot of government land, somewhere in the vicinity of Bet-Shean. Our dream was to establish a Jewish settlement in Jiftlik, at the hub of the Jordan Valley, in the heart of the Arab district by the Adam bridge which connected Shechem with Transjordan. Our spirits were high: the founding of a new kibbutz in a particularly difficult and dangerous spot; the possible award of 3000 dunams of government land which would come into Jewish hands. I knew that if I raised my hand in approval of that plan I would be taking the first step toward my final break with Kefar Tavor. I was fully conscious, but heavy-hearted, when I raised my hand. However, at that stage we weren't required to do anything yet, since we had to wait for the mandatory government's decision regarding the allotment of the land. I won't say I was happy when that decision was delayed, but I wasn't sorry that my unavoidable talk with Papa, the talk I dreaded, could be put off for the time being.

The government's reply was slow in coming. We began to doubt if it ever would come. In the meanwhile we were informed that the initial settlement group destined for Ginosar was about to take possession of its land on the shore of the Sea of Galilee, and it was in urgent need of reinforcements. Encouraged by *Hanoar Haoved*, a youth movement, we decided to fill out the Ginosar group. The inevitable was at hand; the blow which I had so wished to postpone, or lighten, was about to land. I found a spot where I could be alone and worked out various phrases by means of which I hoped to convince Papa that my choice was the right one. I prayed he'd understand and accept the reasons which had moved me to make such a crucial decision for both him and me. I knew how he looked forward to my return and how many hopes he'd pinned on the agricultural and technical knowledge I'd acquired at Kaduri. He believed that with the aid of that knowledge I'd be able to revitalize the farm, whose branches would be modernized upon my return: new breeds, a modern method of crop rotation, and improvements in the cattle barn. During one of our talks he even went so far as to tell me, with great tact, that when I came back home and took over the farm, he didn't intend to intervene in its management. "You'll be the manager," he said and added: "I'll be happy to help you any way you want."

I imagine Papa was plagued by doubts as to whether it had not been his strong, dominating and sometimes heavy-handed personality which had prompted his sons to leave Kefar Tavor, if it had not been his huge shadow which had chased them so far, in order to develop personalities of their own. I don't believe that was why my brothers left. But it was undoubtedly the reason for his prudence with me. He did everything he could to keep me at home on his land, to which he was wedded in such anguish and which he had served with all the might and power of his great love. Now I had to go and tell him that even this final dream of his was only a dream, and that even the youngest of his brood was about to leave the nest; that there was not only an end to his hopes for a Paicovitch tribe on the land of Um-Agabl, but also a considerable doubt as to whether a single Paicovitch would remain on the land with the founder of the dynasty, which had broken up before becoming a dynasty. I loved the Paicovitch land, the village of my birth, the fields and scenes to which I had such vivid, powerful ties; and I loved my father, and admired his flinty, sensitive personality. I knew there was no way out, that I had to do it, because my reason and my aspiration to be among the founders of a new, young kibbutz were no less determined and single-minded. Wavering between my love for him and the dictates of reason, between my duty to him and my aspiration, I was subject to the most agonizing kind of soul-searching.

The time came to break the bad news to him. On a day which hadn't been provided for visits at home, I saddled my horse and galloped off to Kefar Tavor.

"Has anything happened?" he asked anxiously.

"Not yet, but something might," I replied.

I dismounted in silence, tied my horse to the pole and we went over to the porch. We sat down. All the phrases I'd worked out, all the prologues I'd prepared in advance took wing, and I simply began to talk, with no roundabout preliminaries, about my decision to go to the kibbutz. I expected him to object, to insist that I reconsider, but he didn't make a sound. With his eyes on mine and his head slightly bowed, he sat across from me and listened to the verdict. There was a thick silence between us—I don't know if it lasted a few minutes or many, but it seemed a long, long time to me. Then all at once he raised his head and said:

"You're old enough to decide where you're going. I didn't ask my father what to do either. I'm staying here!"

Bewildered and embarrassed, I remarked, without any foundation, that in another year or two, when the first kibbutz buildings were completed, he could join me. He wouldn't let me continue and interrupted:

"Can you picture me anywhere else but Kefar Tavor? Can you imagine me as a kibbutznik?"

His tone as he pronounced the word "kibbutznik" suggested, if not utter scorn, then a definite allusion to something that held a rank rather below his own, that of the free, independent farmer. In such a mood I couldn't tell him that the kibbutz way of life, its objectives, its social concepts and spiritual horizons were no less cherished by me than his independent farm and status were by him. I preferred to keep still, and that was the end of our talk.

◈ ◈

A few weeks remained before my graduation from Kaduri. I promised my father that before joining my classmates who were going to set out shortly afterwards for Ginosar, I would return to the farm in order to finish up the harvesting and plowing. And so I did. However, I was still busy gathering the grain and storing it in the granary when Papa fell ill. It was feared that he had typhus, and though the riots of 1937 were on and traveling was dangerous, we decided to take him to the government hospital in Haifa. Moshe, Eliav and Devorah were in Haifa, and they could support him in his illness. I got in touch with them and together we decided to try and persuade him to move out of Kefar Tavor and go to live with one of them, whomever he preferred; we decided to explain to him that his livelihood was guaranteed: he'd have his own room and would be able to spend his old age in the midst of his big family. None of us were sure we really would succeed in persuading him—I myself was quite pessimistic about it—but we determined to have a try.

Meanwhile I finished in the granary and it was time for me to join my classmates, who had settled in Ginosar. But how could I leave the house without anybody in it, and the farm, when Papa lay ill in Haifa? Some inner voice told me that if I didn't leave it now, I never would.

Then I came to the decision which I consider one of the most difficult and daring I ever made: to dispose of the farm. Such was my intention but I informed no one of it, not my brothers and not my sister and certainly not Papa, who was sick in bed. I was afraid that if they learned of it they would try to prevent me from carrying it out. I was nineteen and Papa seventy. I knew about his stubbornness but also about the loneliness he was in for if he was to remain alone in Kefar Tavor.

Fervently, with an inexplicable zeal and without any second thoughts, I got down to work. I sold everything, the grain, cows, chickens, whatever needed food, water and care. My decision was made alone and therefore it never occurred to me to sell the land itself. I was acquainted with the traders and the agents and I got good prices. Every time I sold a cow or disposed of another hundred chickens, I felt I was drawing nearer to my object. In the end the farm was entirely empty of livestock and I was left with nothing but a wagon, a pair of mules and a year's supply of barley for them. I harnessed the mules to the wagon, loaded it with the plow and the barley and set out for my brother Zvi's place in Netanyah. I intended to ask him to find some profitable work for the mules in the young citrus groves of his settlement, Netanyah, which in those days was a strictly agricultural town. I figured that on the money those draft animals would take in, Papa could live quite well, whether in Kefar Tavor or with one of my brothers or at my sister's home. I hoped with all my heart that once it became clear to him that he had nowhere else to go, he'd prefer to live with one of his children.

I left Kefar Tavor early in the morning. The wagon made its way to Afula, rolling down the road which was no longer so bumpy. But my heart was heavy and the riots were in full swing and that solitary journey was anything but a pleasure trip. From Afula I set out for Haifa. Towards evening I steered my wagon into Kefar-Chassidim, stopping at the home of Rabinovitch, whose son Yehoshua had been one of the initial group of settlers at Ginosar. After a hearty meal, I went to sleep and set out again at dawn. In a few hours the wagon reached Haifa. At the western railroad terminal where Eliav held the post of manager, I got off the wagon and tied the mules to a telephone pole.

"What are you doing here?" he asked in amazement.

I told him I'd just arrived from Kefar Tavor, which made him angrier with me than he'd ever been: "That was irresponsible," he shouted, "and needlessly risky." But when I told him I'd disposed of the farm and he would have to decide how to break the news to Papa, his eyes widened, his face flushed and he was beside himself with rage. In spite of his great love for me he couldn't control his temper. He ran straight for the telephone and summoned Moshe, who was his superior and worked in an adjoining building, in the main office. Moshe arrived and took a good look at the wise guy who had had the nerve to sell the farm all by himself, leaving nothing but a wagon, a pair of mules, a few sacks of barley and some tools. In brief, it was quite a spectacle.

After they had poured out their wrath on me, it naturally became clear to them that the deed could not be undone and there was no sense in crying over spilt milk. Like it or not, they took it upon themselves to prepare Papa for the "good news." Once again I set out, this time down the seacoast in the direction of Binyamina, where I intended to make another stop. Mordechai's reaction wasn't very different from that of my brothers in Haifa, but the greatest amazement at my deed was registered by my brother in Netanyah: not only had I failed to consult him but I had also made him entirely responsible for the care of the remaining animals and their profitable employment. From my brothers' reactions I could see how far I'd gone in deciding to dispose of a farm which had been built up day by day, year after year, for so many decades of suffering and devotion.

With a heavy heart, I took the bus back to Haifa, afraid to come face to face with Papa. In the hospital corridor, my sister and two brothers were waiting for me.

"How did he take it?" I anxiously asked.

And then I was told, to my great surprise, that when Moshe informed him of what I'd done, Papa hadn't complained or been angry; he had just been silent a minute, and then he said to my brother:

"And you let him travel alone at such a time?"

"He's been asking about you every day," my sister went on, "trying to find out if you've come back safe. Or if there's any news of you and when you're supposed to return."

I was very relieved. Once again I witnessed Papa's magnanimity and his love for me. I went in to him; he looked at me without a word of reproach, and though I'm sure he was quite incensed about what I'd done, he made no mention of it. As I went up to his bed he embraced me, stroking my face, and if he refrained from kissing me it was only on account of his illness. All the while his hand never left mine and I could sense his happiness upon seeing me safe and sound at the adventure's end.

The great feud was over. With a lightened heart I boarded the bus for Kefar Tavor. It was half-full of freight, with passengers in the other half. I entered the desolate yard, the vacant house. I couldn't fall asleep all that night, my last in the village of my birth, which I was to leave the next day. Morning found me walking down to the Nazareth-Tiberias road. A truck approached and stopped. The road led on to Ginosar, with no way back.

Chapter 14

PAPA RECOVERED from his illness and did exactly as we feared: he returned to Kefar Tavor, to his liquidated farm and empty home. Alone, at the age of seventy, he began to reconstruct the farm. He cultivated the grain fields with the aid of hired hands. He didn't restock the barn, but he wouldn't give up on the poultry, which he raised mainly for his own consumption. He began a new feud, a kind of war of nerves between him and me: who would go over to which side? Would I return to him, as he must have secretly hoped, once the initial luster of kibbutz "stockade and tower" life had dimmed, or would he join me once he was convinced that Ginosar was my permanent home?

We went on meeting regularly enough especially when in 1938, as the bloody riots and encounters with the Arab gangs reached a peak, I was put in charge of the mobile patrol of the Settlement Police, and the vehicle at my disposal gave me freedom of movement. The Settlement Police was a division of the field companies and I held two ranks: that of sergeant, in keeping with my official British uniform, and that of a company commander in FOSH, an internal commission which I received from the *Hagana* staff. It was part of my duty to look in on Kefar Tavor now and then, but my visits exceeded the official requirements. The fact is that I never missed a chance to see Papa again and catch a glimpse of the village I loved and would continue to love. Papa had many questions about what was going on at Ginsosar, taking a particular interest in the dispute which had erupted between Ginsosar and PICA; as an old campaigner with a lot of experience on that front, he advised us not to give in to them by any means but to keep up the struggle till victory was ours.

In 1939 I resigned my post in the Settlement Police and became the commander of the N.C.O. school which was located at Guara, near En-Hashofet. I kept in touch with Papa from there too. Later I was appointed an instructor in a nationwide platoon leaders' course at Yavniel, cutting down on the distance between us. With the aid of the motorcycle which the *Hagana* staff put at my disposal, I was able to visit him frequently, dining with him and sometimes even staying for the night. He was happy to see me stretch out on the bed alongside his. I can't say for certain if he had already relinquished all hope of bringing me back home by then, but even if he hadn't he never mentioned the matter and never tried to persuade me to return. In our meetings he was full of kindness for me, taking the trouble to prepare my favorite dishes, the ones from our joint bachelors' kitchen, and entertaining me with his good spirits and the charm of his instructive stories. It was a new kind of intimacy which now formed between us, that of two mature, experienced men. I've already mentioned that my father knew how to tell a good story and loved it, but I haven't mentioned another characteristic of his, the faculty for listening to others, which had its origin not only in his upbringing but also in his human, insatiable curiosity. That faculty of his undoubtedly contributed to the deepening of our relationship. I loved to listen to him and was happy to have him share my thoughts and doings.

He witnessed many of them himself, for example the affair of the forty-three *Hagana* prisoners who were jailed in Akko.

The platoon leaders' course in Yavniel was in full swing when we were informed by the *Hagana* intelligence service that its existence had become known to the British secret police, and we could expect a search and arrests at any moment. With the high command's approval, the instructors' staff decided on a quick transfer of the course from Yavniel to Guara. The fastest way to transfer the men and equipment was by bus or truck, but that would have been too obvious and risky, so it was proposed that only the gear would be transported by road, together with a few instructors, while the cadets themselves with the rest of the instructors would go on foot. The route was set so that we would arrive in En-Harod the first night, and after resting during the day, we would proceed to Guara; however, there was a hitch in that plan: about two dozen (I don't remember exactly how many) of the more than sixty cadets served as sergeants and corporals in the Jewish Settlement Police. Needless to say, their participation in the course was illegal. They wore the uniform of the Mandatory government, and if they were caught, they would not only be in for special punishment but the government would also have some questions to ask about the future of the Settlement Police.

It must be remembered that the Second World War had just begun and our national institutions were engaged in a difficult struggle in favor of drafting the Jewish youth, who wanted to volunteer for the fight against the Nazi enemy in the ranks of the British army. Therefore the commander of the course and his deputy—Rafael Lev and Moshe Karmel—decided to transfer all the Settlement Police sergeants in the course separately. I was put in charge of the independent body and it was my mission to bring them safely to Guara. We were also supposed to reach En-Harod on foot, taking a parallel course to the main group, but at a distance. I accepted the mission willingly but on one condition: that I be allowed to depart on the night march from Kefar Tavor and not Yavniel, because (1) I wanted to move the "problematic" group out of Yavniel at once; (2) I wanted to keep as far away as possible from the hubbub created by the larger group's departure; (3) knowing how important it was to transfer the cadre of the Settlement Police safely, I preferred to be my own boss, in other words in close cooperation with the main body but at a distance from it.

My proposal was accepted. I assembled the men, put them on a truck covered with canvas, and we set out for Kefar Tavor. Before long we had disappeared into my father's yard. We weren't scheduled to leave till sundown and in the meanwhile Papa took pains to entertain us, offering us all the treasures of his pantry: eggs, vegetables, fruit and milk; he was short of nothing but bread, which he went to borrow from our good neighbor, Shosheh.

At nightfall I said goodbye to my father. He embraced me and if I'm not mistaken, he also kissed me on the cheek.

"Be careful," he told me as we set out, "there's not a single Jewish settlement from here to En-Harod. The pipeline is guarded by the Arab Border Force. Don't take any risks."

"It'll be all right, Papa," I blurted and the column straightened out, with me in the lead.

We had set our rendezvous with the main force, which was supposed to depart from Yavniel, at a spot not far from the ridge overlooking the Harod Valley. We had no wireless communication and I relied on my familiarity with the lay of the land. We advanced according to plan in an orderly night march, constantly on the alert. Equipped with firearms, hand grenades and first-aid pouches, we were resolved to escape any police patrol we might encounter, even opening fire if necessary in order to cover our retreat.

The police sergeants in my unit came from all over the country and most of them were unfamiliar with the area of our march, but their excellent training had prepared them for the difficult route. At two o'clock in the morning we reached the rendezvous point, as marked on the map. At once we took up defense positions, posting spotters in anticipation of the main force which according to plan was to arrive any minute. Two hours passed, two hours which were seemingly endless, and there was not a trace of the main force. I was worried: if I was to remain in that hostile, patrol-infested area I would put my men in jeopardy, and therefore it might be better for us to go on before sunrise, especially since the object of my mission was to bring them to a safe place; on the other hand, if we were to move out and the main force was to arrive at the rendezvous and not find us, they might conclude that we hadn't arrived yet and wait for us, thus putting themselves in danger. I was sorry we'd set the rendezvous at that spot and no less sorry about the whole idea of a rendezvous; it would have been better for each force to proceed independently to the objective, on a separate path.

Unwittingly I recalled Papa's parting words, as we left his yard: "Why do you have to meet on the way? You should meet at En-Harod, it's safer."

The hours dragged on, heavy with tension. And then, after much deliberation, I decided to put one of the sergeants in charge of the unit and order him to lead it to En-Harod while I waited alone for the main force. I summoned Sergeant Arieh Eshel (later one of the senior officials in the Israeli Foreign Office and our ambassador to Brazil and Canada; he passed away a few years ago), and I appointed him my deputy and the leader of the force. I explained the route of advance to him, through the hollow leading from the highland to the valley, so that the marchers would be well hidden. As I whispered my final orders to him—time was pressing since dawn had arrived sooner than I'd expected—I saw one of the spotters crawling towards me. He informed me that he'd noticed suspicious movements a few hundred meters to the east. I slipped down to the spotting position and discovered, in what was already the clear light of morning, a unit of the Border Force which surrounded a group of men in Jewish attire. I was certain that this was the main body which had failed to arrive. Now there was no room for doubt: I couldn't tarry and endanger the sergeants. I had to get them out of there no matter what. Those were my orders and I had to act accordingly. Moving quickly, half-crawling and half-sliding, we disappeared into the hollow and then made for En-Harod in double time.

I informed the district command of what had happened, quickly got in touch with the general staff and was ordered to move out of En-Harod, for fear of a search, but not to Guara; the sergeants, I was told, must return at once by the shortest possible route to their posts and sign in at their precincts, in order to cover up for their absence. It was feared that word of the sergeants' participation in the course would reach the British, and their signatures in the registers would furnish them with alibis.

I remained in En-Harod all day in order to keep track of what happened to the forty-three cadets. I hoped that through local connections and with the aid of several government officials who were not partial to the Arabs, I might succeed in obtaining their release. The next day I went to Afula, visited the town manager and asked him to ring up my father and tell him I was all right. Now I had to make contact with the proper parties in order to organize the legal defense of the forty-three prisoners, who had meanwhile been transferred to the Akko jail. I was at home in that prison, since people from Ginosar were doing time there as well, those with whom I had participated in guard duty over the water sources of the kibbutz. (That battle had ended with the death of the neighboring village chief and the wounding of two other Arabs. My buddies in the battle were all in the Settlement Police, and I had escaped arrest because I wau no longer in that force and my name did not appear in the police register.) During the time of their sentence I regularly visited my kibbutz buddies in prison, accompanied by M. Aliash and Y. S. Shapira, the lawyers provided for them by the *Hagana*. In that way, under the pretext of visiting my buddies from Ginosar, I was admitted to the Akko jail only a single day after the arrest of the forty-three cadets. The commander of the course, Rafael Lev, his deputy, Moshe Karmel, and the instructors, Moshe Dayan and Yaakov Salomon, told me how they'd been caught by a unit of the Arab Border Force. The entire story has been published as a book by Moshe Karmel, *Forty-Three Letters From a Hebrew Prisoner.*

◈ ◈

Papa's health took a turn for the worse and he was sick again. Like it or not, he agreed to move in with my sister, "but only for the time being," as he put it. As the days passed he gradually got used to the idea that he would have to remain there. Another year went by. My sister wrote me that although Papa was feeling well he didn't take to city life, and she wrote again that he missed me and talked of me a great deal. I knew that the only way to make up for his loss of Kefar Tavor would be to resettle him in some other village environment. Once again, I prepared nothing in advance and declined to say anything to my brothers and sister, talking the matter over with

Ruth alone, who encouraged me to go ahead. I turned to the commander of the Galilee district, Nachum Shadmi—this was in the beginning of 1940—and asked him to lend me his car; I drove to my sister's place in Haifa, told Papa I wanted him to come with me to Ginosar, and to stress the point I read him the unanimous decision of the kibbutz's general meeting which invited him to settle among us. There was a pause, and after a few minutes he said:

"How did you know when to come?"

"I had the feeling it was the right time," I replied.

"Yes. It's the right time," he answered; "I'll go with you, but tell me, is Ginosar your home? Are you sure of it? I've already deserted my lands twice, in Machanaim and Kefar Tavor. I don't want to move another time."

I knew that his departure from Machanaim and Kefar Tavor had left open, aching wounds in his heart. I promised Papa he wouldn't have to move any more. I packed his belongings in the car and in two hours we were in Ginosar.

Till his cabin was finished we gave him our little room, two meters by three in size, while we settled back down in a tent, as we had during our first days in Ginosar. Papa objected to this. He had no wish to oust us from our room, even temporarily, and, moreover, he couldn't accept the idea that his daughter-in-law, whom he affectionately called "my daughter," should be living in a tent, exposed to the heat by day and the chill of night, while he, as he put it, "wallowed in a royal palace." Ruth convinced him that considering Ginosar's climate and our youthful age, there could be no more romantic and pleasing place to live than in a tent by the Sea of Galilee.

He took a liking to the place and struck up a friendship with the senior members, but even so there was a painful side to his adaptation to the kibbutz way of life. All at once the roles were changed: in Kefar Tavor he had been

the master of the household and the owner of the farm and I was his son and prodigy, whereas at Ginosar he was Yigal's father whom the kibbutz had taken in. Whenever his health permitted he would work, particularly in the little garden next to his house, but the farm area was also within his province. The rapid progress and the modern scientific and technical methods which went into our agricultural work made a great impression on him; nevertheless, he didn't refrain from finding fault with imperfections as he saw them. For example, he couldn't bear the speck of negligence which was an inevitable part of almost any farm work on the kibbutz, nor could he put up with such trifles as pieces of wood which were left lying around, or the bad habit of not returning tools and other implements to the storeroom once they were no longer in use. Innocently wandering about the yard, he had more than one occasion to express his displeasure at the sight of a wooden board with a nail stuck in it, its dangerous point facing up; at times I found him in some neglected spot, tidying it up without having been asked—he had the watchful eye of a real proprietor who cannot and will not change his ways, even in retirement.

As I've said, he was critical of one thing and another in the kibbutz, but he had a great admiration for its solidarity. One time he jestingly told me: "I still have to find out how kibbutz members feel in middle age, but there's no doubt that the kibbutz is a paradise for the very young and the very old." Here too his perceptivity stood him in good stead, since it's absolutely certain that for children and teenagers one could not imagine a freer or happier environment than that provided by the togetherness of the kibbutz, whose society developed a particular concern, second to none, for the needs of its children and adolescents. And as for social security and one's ability to find himself a place in old age as well, it's doubtful if anyone could imagine a more ideal situation than that of the old people on the kibbutz. The well-being of those two age groups needed no further proof as far as he was concerned; however, he was far from certain about the feelings of the kibbutz member who had already exhausted his capacity for physical labor but had yet to reach old age. To the very last, he never took a definite position on that subject.

In Ginosar he also went on walking his usual five kilometers a day. Every day at sundown he would don his peaked cap, take his cane and march out in that easy, measured pace of his along the country paths or the roadside. "Walking is good for your health," he would say, "and it gives you a chance to do some clear thinking." On one of those walks he found himself involved in a skirmish with some Arabs, the last one of his life. I heard about it from Zerrubavel Ben-Nur, one of the old-timers at Ginosar:

"It was in the summer of 1955. By then Papa was in his eighties. All the members of the kibbutz were at the wedding of the son of one of the friendly local Arabs. He was the only one who remained in the kibbutz. Towards evening he went out on his regular walk and also to keep an eye on our watermelon field by the highway. Approaching the field, he spotted two young Arabs aged eighteen or so who had seized the opportunity to filch some watermelons. He let them get about their work and surprised them from the rear. In a thundering voice he ordered them to put their hands up. They froze on the spot, with their hands raised. At once he commanded them to fold their hands behind their backs, which they did. He took some cords they had on them, tied them up and marched them off to the kibbutz yard. There he put them in the storeroom, locked the door and waited for the military commander of the kibbutz to return."

◈ ◈

At Ginosar, much to his chagrin, he renewed his contacts with the PICA officials after a separation which had lasted many years. It goes without saying which side he was on in our struggle with the organization which he regarded, if not with utter disapproval, then with mixed feelings at the very least. Our struggle had reached the stage at which PICA decided to take legal action in order to get a notice of eviction which would allow it to remove us from the premises. My father was afraid that the organization might win out in court, not because justice was on its side but by virtue of the means it was liable to employ in order to clinch the case in advance. One day, when I went with Ruth to his room for a cup of tea, he said: "I think the trial is going to be called off."

"How do you know?" I asked him.

He replied: "This morning when I went out for a stroll in the woods, I met Mr. X from the PICA office in Haifa. He came to look the place over and he complained to me about the senior members of Ginosar, especially you. In his opinion, you're all violating the law and offending PICA's honor. Mr. X asked me to help him persuade you to accept the organization's proposal and move out to another settlement site."

"And what did you tell him?" I asked.

"What did I tell him? I told him: It's a good thing I met you, Mr. X, because after all you know that out of all those rats at PICA I've always respected you as an honest man, so, Mr. X, I think it's my personal obligation to warn you about the risk you're running. . . . What risk? asked Mr. X, so I told him I'd heard that PICA was going to take Ginosar to court and the kibbutz members had decided that if Ginosar lost the case they'd retaliate by executing a few PICA officials, and you're one of them. So you'd better drop your charges."

"And you really believe that threat is enough to make them back down?"

"I believe they cherish their lives more than their control of Ginosar's lands," replied Papa and added, "I don't think there's going to be a trial."

view from my window

There wasn't, and to this day I don't know why it was called off, but Papa was sure to the very last that by circulating that threat, which was utterly unfounded, he had played a decisive role in Ginosar's history. Of course he knew we would never employ the violent means with which he had frightened Mr. X, but apparently he had decided to use the threat thinking that if it wouldn't help us, it certainly wouldn't hurt.

Chapter 15

I'VE ALREADY told about Papa's initial meeting with Yitzhak Sadeh, which was followed by many others, in Kefar Tavor at first and later at Ginosar. Yitzhak, with his talent for human relations, treated Papa with a respect which sometimes seemed even overdone to me. Every now and then he brought him a bottle of vodka, and since neither of them were teetotalers they would toast one another and converse in the warm, friendly atmosphere which always prevailed during their meetings. At times, for my father's gratification, the old man would also speak my praises. With his many-sided personality, Yitzhak knew how to attract people and be attracted to them as well, and I was happy about the bond which formed between the two old men who loved and respected one another.

By virtue of my authority and activities, my father was, as they say, in the know. In 1941, when the *Palmach** was established, my father was already living in Ginosar and thus he had a chance to observe the inauguration ceremony in the eucalyptus grove on the shore of the Sea of Galilee, the grove which went down in history. He frequently visited the grove to watch the Palmach's "A" company, my own, during its training, drilling and camp-

* The shock force of the *Hagana*.

fires. On more than one occasion he sat about the campfire with us, a little to one side, listening to our talks and songs. Sometimes, when he was familiar with the melody, he would join in with us in a soft hum. Thanks to his natural gift of tact, he always kept within bounds and was never a bother to those about him.

Though raised on nineteenth-century literature, he thought and lived in accordance with contemporary concepts, those of the national revival and redemption; he had no use for flowery language, and therefore I was rather surprised when he said to me one day: "Yigal, has it ever occurred to you that as the commander of the first company of the *Palmach*, you're the commander of the first company of the first independent Hebrew army since the time of Bar-Kokba?"

I had no less of a historical consciousness than he, but that remark of his really astounded me, since it wasn't in keeping with his usual manner of expression and his plain, practical kind of talk.

Papa regarded the *Palmach* with utter seriousness while we were a bit contemptuous of ourselves, with the typical lightheadedness of the young. He excitedly kept track of our training and was thrilled by the level of our exercises, our daring jumps and night actions. At times he would say to me: "We never knew about that. If we had only known how to do that in our day . . . oho! Who knows how far we would have gone!"

He followed the *Palmach*'s growth intimately because he saw it as something of major political and military importance, a real historic feat, and also because I was involved in it from its very inception. My world became his and throughout the years he kept track of my activities. And I used to let him share them as much as possible and tell him everything that might be of interest to him. He was a witness to the political arguments and struggles, particularly those pertaining to the partition of the country. On the one hand, he was unwilling to go along with us in relinquishing half of the Land of Israel, and he stuck to his claim that we had already given up more than half the country anyway, when the Kingdom of Transjordan was founded; but on the other hand he was skeptical of the Jewish community's ability to get the better of the British. In his opinion, which he directed at me too, we had underestimated the power of the empire which was apparently determined to thwart the national aspirations of the Jewish population in the country. He was reconciled to our struggle against the British and anxiously followed each of our actions, but he pinned no great hopes on them. He would hide his concern when parting from me before an operation, but his joy was plain to see when he met me on my return, safe and sound. He was afraid the British might jail me with a heavy sentence.

A good part of my activities—both during the struggle against the British and in the first stages of the War of Liberation—took place in the north, and thus I was able to come home often enough. I would generally return at dawn, and without hesitating or looking at my watch I'd knock on his door and go in to wish him a good morning. And those really were good mornings in Papa's room. With a bright, happy expression he would get up and make a cup of tea, sometimes taking out a bottle of arrack as well so that we could drink a toast to a successful operation. He and Ruth took to one another very well and he never felt isolated when I was away from home, though my days of absence increased as we approached the second, critical stage of the War of Liberation—the stage of open war with the Arab countries.

My tasks kept me farther and farther away from home but I always did my best to keep in touch with him, whether by sending him notes or my spoken regards as conveyed by some friend who happened to stop off at Ginosar, or through the newspapers, which was also a way of keeping in touch, even if the contact was indirect and impersonal. Alert and concerned, he kept track of the war's development and especially my part in it.

In April 1948, when I was put in command of "Operation Yiftach," which was meant to liberate the Upper Galilee and raise the siege on Safed, which was fighting for its life, I stopped off at Ginosar to see him and my family and friends. I spent some three hours in his company and throughout our talk he repeatedly stressed the strategic importance of Mount Canaan. He had a powerful love for that mountain and the scenic prospects it afforded. Was it because long ago, on one of its slopes, he had met a girl riding a donkey, the girl who was to be his wife? But now he didn't talk about the mountain's beautiful views but rather its importance as the central commanding height which allowed the one who controlled it to control the entire Upper Galilee.

◈ ◈

The battles for the liberation of the Galilee were on. Though they were waged far from Papa's home, their reverberations were easily heard there. Later he told me that during the decisive battle for Safed, with the detonations rumbling down Mount Canaan and up to Ginosar, he had sat outside his room all the while and tried to guess by the sounds what the military situation was like and what I was personally experiencing under the stress of battle. The capture of Safed gave birth to a pretty tale which has to do with me, but if I quote it here it's only because it would be too bad to miss such a fine story. Dr. Yaakov Harozen writes:

"The liberation of the Galilee has been fully described in books about the War of Liberation. But in the alleyways of Safed, tales went around for many days afterwards about the city's miraculous salvation. The Jewish elders recalled that the young general, Yigal, was the grandson of Rabbi Alter Shwartz from Safed, the paragon of pioneers who had left home and gone off to Jeona, in order to build it up, together with his friends, as Gai-Oni. Thus the city of *Haari*, the saintly kabbalist, was privileged to be redeemed by Yigal, the commander of Safed extraction.

"At the same time, the pious women of the holy city proudly depicted the *Palmach* troops and their officers as righteous saviors, and they gave free rein to their imagination in explaining how the miracle of Safed had occurred. Simply enough, all the holy dwellers of the burial ground had risen from their graves (some of the Safed women had even heard the stir they made when leaving their place of rest), and after appearing for the roll call they joined the troops at war. Every *Palmach* soldier was escorted by two of the great men of Israel, who lovingly guarded him. At the same time a dozen of the most righteous of the righteous flocked to Yigal and sheltered him on every side (even an armored tank couldn't have kept him safer), and among the defenders was Rabbi Alter Shwartz from Safed, side by side with Rabbi Yosef Karo. No wonder that Safed prevailed and those who had plotted against it took flight like rabbits!" *

In the War of Liberation I also had my share of perplexing situations, the nature and causes of which are not within the compass of this book. At times I would tell my father about a few of my uncertainties, but I refrained from making him a party to many of my disappointments. One disappointment of mine stemmed from the rejection of a plan which I had proposed immediately after the termination of "Operation Yiftach." It was a plan to concen-

* *Chazon Habitnachalut Bagalil*, page 364.

trate a mobile force under my command in order to execute a deep flanking movement from the Bet-Shan Valley through the Jordan Valley, towards Jericho. It had a twofold objective: to cut off the Arab Legion and the Iraqi Expeditionary Force from the east bank of the Jordan, and also to reach Jerusalem from the rear, in cooperation, of course, with the Israeli forces on the western side, which would apply concurrent pressure.

"Don't worry," Papa told me, "Jerusalem won't run away, you'll get there from another direction."

A more painful disappointment occurred in June and July 1948, after "Operation Dani," which saw us liberating the cities of Lod and Ramla, raising the siege on Jewish Jerusalem for the last time and broadening the corridor which led to the capital. At that time the high command of the security department decided to divide the country into fronts. I was very eager to be put in charge of the central front, which would include Jerusalem. I wanted to command the operation which was to liberate the whole city of Jerusalem and I believed in the possibility of it. With that objective in mind, I even formulated an entire strategic theory, the "fan" theory, according to which the initial breakthrough should be made in the center, with the thrusts on the flanks coming afterwards. I had faith in that theory and its practical results, but my request to be appointed commander of the central front was not granted. I was put in command of the southern front.

When I told Papa about that, he said, "I'm all for the Old City of Jerusalem, but the Negev can live without it and Jerusalem can't without the Negev. Take the command of the Negev in good spirits. I'm sure you'll get to the capital from the Negev." And the fact is that when I was appointed commander of the southern front I put in a proposal to capture Jerusalem and the entire west bank by means of a mighty pincers movement from the north and south, with me commanding the southern arm. Unfortunately, that proposal of mine was also rejected, to be followed by our lamentation for having lost the chance forever. Papa was quite incensed by the way the war ended, both from a territorial and a political standpoint.

Now, after the pessimistic spell he had been in at the beginning of the war, he was exceptionally confident regarding the results of the campaign and the possibilities before us.

I went down to the Negev. He saw the capture of Beer-Sheva, a city with which he had been familiar since his Turkish army days, as the crowning achievement of the entire War of Liberation, it being no light matter that the capital of the Negev had fallen into our hands and his son had overseen its capture. My father's heart swelled with pride. One day I received a note, a plain piece of paper on which was written, in pencil: "My congratulations on the capture of Beer-Sheva. There you have the main crossroads of the Negev and can go on to liberate the rest. But permit me to draw your attention to a place we used to call Bir-Asloj, south of Beer-Sheva, on the road to Sinai. You have a fresh spring there and a mountainous formation which is easy to defend. If you don't hold Bir-Asloj, Beer-Sheva will be in danger. I advise you to take Bir-Asloj soon."

As destiny or chance decreed, that note reached me as we were making ready for the attack on Bir-Asloj. I showed it to my operations officer, Yitzhak Rabin, and said, "Well, Yiṭzhak, we have to carry out Papa's order and capture Bir-Asloj."

At our next meeting, when I told him that the capture of Bir-Asloj had really been vital and his plan was strategically sound, he couldn't have been happier.

◈ ◈

We weren't always in agreement about everything, not even on political matters. When I got out of the army, he didn't conceal his doubts about my taking such a step. Of course he knew of my disappointments, and he used to say, like a suspicious farmer, "Ben-Gurion can't bear to share the victory with anyone. That's why he disbanded your *Palmach*, and he'll be happier with you out of uniform." But when I told him the circumstances which had compelled me to resign, he agreed with me, saying, "The preservation of one's honor is more important than his position, no matter how high that may be."

◈ ◈

On the most difficult, hectic days I would make a special effort to be with my father, to see him and talk with him. Of course this was in line with another aspiration: to seize every opportunity to spend time with my family and meet my fellow members in the kibbutz. I made it a practice to do so in all stages of my military and public activities, as a member of the Settlement Police, FOSH and the *Palmach*, as an active participant in the *Hagana* and the Israeli army, as a Knesset member and minister.

I spent a whole year in Syria, from the beginning to the end of 1942. With the collaboration of the Jewish Agency and the *Palmach* staff, I was sent there as an agent of the British army. My official position was that of supervisor for the construction company *Solel-Boneh* in Syria and the Lebanon, a fine disguise, but the missions in which I was engaged as an officer in the Arab platoon were of a strictly military, underground nature. I had a car at my disposal and would regularly drop in at home, taking the fastest and shortest route, from Damascus via the Benot-Yaakov Bridge, even if it was only for a few hours. I never missed a family event, whether in Ginosar or at the home of one of my brothers. Even from Aleppo in the north of Syria I would arrive in Ginosar in order to drive Papa to Haifa, Binyamina or Netanyah, which we generally used to reach by way of Tsemach, Bet-Shan, Jenin, Shechem and Tul-

Karem. I believe Papa really felt my attachment to him, and that's also why he agreed to join me in Ginosar.

A special part in his adaptation to life in Ginosar was played by my wife Ruth. They developed an extraordinary attachment for one another. He, ever dignified and sensitive, was won over by her vivacity and her tactful concern for his needs. She took our children with her to spend their free time in Grandpa's room till they came of their own accord, to listen to his exciting stories. Since I was often away from home owing to my tasks in the underground and on the *Hagana* staff, Ruth was his closest companion. With her he could talk about anything, even the most intimate affairs which he generally kept to himself. As for his grandchildren, he came to see that they did ensure the succession of the Paicovitch clan in spite of everything. His relationship with Ruth was based not only on love but on honor and respect as well. More than once he said with a merry smile and a wink that his youngest son had good taste. He had not only picked the right father but also the right woman, "for himself and me too." He saw his own image in his grandson, Yiftach of the blue eyes and fair hair, while his granddaughter, Goni, with her brown eyes and dark hair, reminded him of his wife, my late mother.

During his first years at Ginosar he never stopped thinking about the possibility of reviving his farm in Kefar Tavor, but little by little he got used to kibbutz life, and he came to see the sense in it too. Even so, I have no doubt that if I'd agreed to go back with him to his village, that would surely have been the greatest compensation I could have ever made to him.

We were in a particularly perplexing situation when I considered the possibility of resigning from the Knesset in order to go to England and continue my studies at Oxford University. He had no hesitations about the choice before me, the Knesset or the university, and he decreed: "Go and study. Scholarship is a permanent asset, and the Knesset won't run away. The more you learn the better you'll be at politics."

"But if I'm gone for two or three years, will you stay here alone?" I said.

His answer to that was: "I won't be alone. I'm living in your kibbutz and I'm sure I'll get along very well in those two years if, of course, you write me from time to time and if you make good progress," he added with a smile. Twice I went abroad to study, twice I left him alone and twice it was he who encouraged me to go.

Chapter 16

ONE DAY it was rumored in Israel that I was invited to return from Oxford in order to take a ministerial post in the government. That was during the fifth term of the Knesset, and the senior kibbutz members went to Papa's room to congratulate him.

"They're nominating your son for minister," the members told him.

"I think it's important to be a minister," Papa replied, "but if he were to take my advice he'd reject the proposal till he's finished with his studies."

Overseas, we also deliberated a good deal as to whether I should accept the invitation from Jerusalem or keep on with my studies till my research was done, but it was actually Ruth, though generally on the side of my studies and in no hurry to return to Israel, who said: "I think Papa would be very pleased to see his son as a member of government."

We returned to Israel and to this day I have a hard time deciding which of the various reasons tipped the balance, but one thing is sure: my thinking about Papa played an important part in my decision to return.

Once we'd embraced and kissed, he asked me:

"Is there any chance you'll be able to finish your thesis someday?"

"I'm afraid not," I answered. "A minister's job demands all the time and energy you have."

Then, after a long pause for thought, he asked, "Are you sure this government can stick it out for four years? If I were in your shoes I'd make sure I had a way to go back to Oxford, in case the government falls."

"There will always be a way back to Oxford for me, Papa, but if this government really is in danger, won't you agree with me that one should do all he can to prevent its fall?"

"Well, your decisions have been the right ones so far," he said and got up. "I hope you're right this time too."

"Have all my decisions been the right ones?" I asked humorously, since I knew I'd disheartened him more than once.

"Yes, all your decisions," he replied.

"Even the decision to join the kibbutz?"

"Yes," he replied, "the way of life you chose has at least one advantage over mine: your kibbutz is your fortress and support. It allows you to study, work and be active within the kibbutz and on the outside too. There's a meaning in kibbutz life that I never knew in mine."

"There's another advantage," I said to him; "thanks to its social structure, its occupational diversity in agriculture, industry and municipal services with an almost unlimited capacity for employment, the kibbutz can do more towards maintaining the family than any other form of life."

"Time will tell," he replied.

There was a definite sadness to that reply, and I thought I heard a trace of the failure to which he was never reconciled, even at the very end: the fading of his dream for the Paicovitch clan on the lands of Kefar Tavor. But then he added, "Actually, the kibbutz is a clan, a very special one."

He was ninety-one years old when he passed away. In his will we discovered that he didn't want to be buried in Kefar Tavor, the village of his great love and bitter disappointment. From the time he left the settlement, he hadn't visited it even once; he simply refused to set foot there. Whenever I took him for a drive and we had to pass by the village on our way to the south of Israel or the central region, he would cover his face with a handkerchief before we drew near his fields and wouldn't remove it till the car was on the far side of Mount Tabor. He was familiar with the curves of the road and he could tell where they were in the dark as well. All his hopes had been centered about that village, and he regarded the forsaking of his lands as his greatest failure, which could neither be forgiven or excused. Only the ones who knew what that man had put into his village could understand how he felt.

We, his sons, did know, and although we buried him in the Binyamina cemetery as he requested in his will, when it came time to choose a stone to mark his grave we went back, Mordechai and I, to Papa's fields in Kefar Tavor and headed for the Kastel plot—the one he had transformed with his own hands from a hill of rocks and thorns to the finest and most fertile of all his lands—and from among the basalt stones in that field we chose a massive black rock which he had once uprooted with his own hands and set as a boundary marker in a corner of his field, and with the aid of a lever mounted on our vehicle the black rock was raised and conveyed by his grandchildren to the cemetery, a tombstone untouched by any mason's hand. Only his name was engraved on it, and two words: A FOUNDER.

On the first anniversary of his death the whole family congregated at his grave, his children, grandchildren and great-grandchildren. There was a hush. Suddenly a voice was heard, belonging to Udi, the youngest of the great-grandchildren: "That rock looks an awful lot like Grandpa."